Talking Steel Towns:
The Men and Women of
America's Steel Valley

Ellie Wymard

For the Carlow University
Library —
Ellie Wymard
11-07

Carnegie Mellon University Press
Pittsburgh 2007

Other books by Ellie Wymard:

Divorced Women, New Lives (Ballantine, 1990)

Men on Divorce (Hay House, 1994)

Conversations With Uncommon Women: Insights from women who've risen above life's challenges to achieve extraordinary success (AMACOM, 1999)

Cover:
LUKE SWANK [Two Boys Overlooking Steel Mill] c. 1927-1935; Gelatin silver print, 5 15/16 x 7 7/8
Courtesy of Carnegie Library of Pittsburgh

Front spread:
BUD HARRIS [Jones & Laughlin Steel Plant in the Hazelwood/Greenfield area] © 1967
Courtesy of Bud Harris

Coda photo:
BUD HARRIS [Man of Iron, Harbison-Walker, Pittsburgh, PA] © 1972
Courtesy of Bud Harris

"Entering the Oven" from *Origins of Evening* by Robert Gibb.
Copyright © 1998 by Robert Gibb. Used by permission of W. W. Norton & Company, Inc.

Book design and layout by Connie Amoroso
Cover design by Erika Holmquist

Library of Congress Control Number: 2006932553
ISBN: 978-0-88748-478-0 cloth
ISBN: 978-0-88748-477-3 pbk.
Copyright © 2007 by Ellie Wymard
All rights reserved
Printed and bound in the United States of America

10   9   8   7   6   5   4   3   2   1

For the memory of Petro and Anna

and their legacy:

Great-grandchildren Josh and Peter

And great-great-grandchildren

Tommy and Jake

Elizabeth, Jack, Gus and Mary

Contents

Acknowledgments

The writing of *Talking Steel Towns* required considerable research and many conversations. With gratitude I acknowledge all of the women and men of America's Steel Valley who talked to me seriously about their lives and gave me great encouragement for this project.

Forever thanks to the staff of the Rivers of Steel National Heritage Area, located in Homestead, Pennsylvania, in the Bost Building, once the headquarters of labor organizers and journalists from all over the world, during the Lockout and Strike of 1892. I was provided mines of information by August R. Carlino, Director; Doris J. Dyan, Ph.D., Director of Cultural Conservation; Ron Baraff, Director of Museum Collections & Archives; Janis L. Dofner, Director of Communications; and archivists Susan Lineback and Julie Williams.

I want to note the rich resources and helpful manner of the staffs of the Carnegie Library of Braddock, the Carnegie Library of Homestead, the Heinz History Center, and the Pennsylvania Department of the Carnegie Library of Pittsburgh.

Special gratitude to Roy G. Dorrance, III, Vice Chairman, U. S. Steel Corporation, for taking me on a necessary journey of Pittsburgh steel mills: Edgar Thomson, the Irvin Works, and Clairton Works. During the tour, Nadine Gurcak's careful notes kept me on course through the eruption of blast furnaces and the heat of coke ovens.

I want to thank Judith Applebaum for her sensitive reading of this manuscript and intelligent suggestions. Because of the enduring friendship and advice of Mary Ann Eckels, the editor of my first book published in 1990 by Ballantine, I continue to persevere through the mysteries of the publishing world.

My eternal gratitude to Mary Cvetan for her thorough research, cheerful disposition, intelligence and wit, but most of all for championing the completion and publication of *Talking Steel Towns*. And also to Mary Jo Benassi whose transcriptions of my interviews were indispensable to my writing.

I truly appreciate that Grace Ann Geibel, RSM, Ph.D., president emerita of Carlow University, believed in this project from day one and encouraged my every step through the Steel Valley. Thanks to Gary Smith, Ph.D., provost of Carlow University, for his keen interest in my stories along the way.

I am enormously grateful to my editor, Cynthia Lamb, for saying "Carnegie Mellon is where this book should be," and guiding it through the publication process. My deep appreciation to Gerald Costanzo, director of the Carnegie Mellon University Press, for knowing that readers from across the United States have roots in the Steel Valley.

And always, I am blessed by the love, encouragement and sustaining enthusiasm of Buddy Wymard, husband *non compare.*

Introduction

꧁ ꧂

From My Grandfather's Grave

My grandfather was crushed to death at Pittsburgh's Edgar Thomson Steel Works when he fell into the rollers that flatten red-hot billets into sheets of steel. His grave is less than ten miles from my home, but I visited it for the first time only recently. I shared this personal moment with two strangers, the manager of the cemetery and one of its gardeners. We carried with us a stiff parchment scroll listing in pen and ink the names of the longtime dead. Holding it down with stones we found in the grass, we carefully paced row 10, division 5 . . . Hornak . . . Kizasonik . . . Buntak. . . . With fingertips, I read the worn letters of his headstone, Petro Buntak (1866-1907). In this act of simple ceremony, I felt in touch with a past I craved to know.

I was pulled to my grandfather's grave, high in the hills of the Steel Valley of Pittsburgh, after teaching an undergraduate course in memoir writing. At the age of sixty, I wanted to reach into my generational past the way my students were able to do.

Petro Buntak is buried at a top rim of the Monongahela Cemetery and looks down on the great mills of Andrew Carnegie and rivers once glutted with barges of iron. These steep slopes, far above flatlands and waterways, were of no use to industry, and so they became burial grounds, especially for immigrant laborers, many of whom died in the rites of making steel. I will never know the details of my grandfather's life and death, but I vowed at his grave to gather the perceptions and stories of other men and women in the Steel Valley before they are also left untold.

In living rooms smothered with Steeler pennants and dining rooms cluttered with memorabilia from visits to the "old country"; in shabby union halls and backyard gardens lush with ripe tomatoes; at scarred library tables under portraits of Andrew Carnegie, and across lattes in Starbucks and Paneras, I listened to hardworking men and women of all ages tell me about their lives. Over kitchen tables, drinking tea and eating Hungarian pastries, I heard many sweet stories.

From the archives of the Rivers of Steel National Heritage Area, in Homestead, Pennsylvania, I read oral histories that have never been published. Families shared their scrapbooks, diaries and letters.

The people of the Steel Valley have very private memories of the mills, many involving loss: husbands, fathers, sons and friends mutilated; families disrupted by strikes and layoffs. Since the future of Pittsburgh is with high technology, higher education and healthcare, some residents are leery about recalling personal memories of an industrial past for fear of reinforcing its image as a dirty steel town. But the men who fired the open hearths and the women who packed their lunches and counted pennies during labor strikes are the heart and soul of America. Their hands shaped this country no less than the words of New England's genteel prophets and poets or the maps charted by westward pioneers. The hot reality of the steel mills needs to be seared into the American consciousness as a permanent reminder of our identity as a nation of immigrants. As easily as the mill sites were reconfigured, memories can fade. To forget the stories of the Steel Valley prior to the closing of the mills is to demean the struggle of all people who sailed to these shores believing in possibilities beyond their circumstances.

Poor young men in Ireland, Scotland, Germany and Eastern Europe left their villages for the steel mills of Andrew Carnegie, hoping to "make it" in America. Carnegie's first plant, Edgar Thomson (ET) in Braddock, was the progenitor of Big Steel when the Bessemer furnace was first fired there in 1875. Two miles west of ET, Carnegie bought the Pittsburgh Bessemer Steel Company in 1883, the plant that later would be known as the Homestead Works, the most famous mill in the world. U. S. Steel, America's first billion-dollar corporation, was founded in 1901 as a merger of Andrew Carnegie and J. P. Morgan. From then, until nearly the end of the twentieth century, industrial plants extended east and west from the city of Pittsburgh and lined river towns up and down the Allegheny, Monongahela and Ohio Rivers. This region was dubbed the "Steel Capital of the World."

At the center of this region in the Monongahela Valley, U. S. Steel plants, with the mystique of pyramids, dominated both sides of the river for twenty-one miles between the South Side of Pittsburgh and east to Clairton. They included the Homestead Works and Carrie Furnace, Edgar Thomson and the Duquesne Works, National Tube, the Irvin Works and Clairton Works. At the height of Big Steel, these mills employed more than 100,000 people.

During World War II, more than 20,000 people at the Homestead Works alone made tanks, ships and bullets. When I attended a meeting of the Steelworkers Organization of Active Retirees (SOAR) at an Elks Club in Homestead, grizzled steelworkers worried about cutbacks with their health insurance, and spoke with great pride of their contributions to the Allied victory: "The war wouldn't have been won without us."

Pittsburgh Steel was used to build the Brooklyn Bridge, the Panama Canal locks, the Empire State Building, Rockefeller Center, the Oakland Bay Bridge, the United Nations and the World Trade Center. The Irvin Works is now the world's major supplier of sheet steel for appliances.

But with the decline of the steel industry in the past twenty years, including the razing of plants and the rusting of company towns, the era of Big Steel is receding further into our national memory. During the 1980s, U. S. Steel shut down American Bridge in Ambridge, plus every plant in the Steel Valley, except for Edgar Thomson, the Clairton Works and Irvin Works, which now employ fewer than six thousand. LTV Steel (formerly Jones & Laughlin) closed its mighty plants in Aliquippa, Hazelwood and Pittsburgh's South Side. Wheeling-Pittsburgh closed its plant in Monessen. Huge manufacturing plants that supplied steel industry products also closed in riverbank towns like McKees Rocks, Neville Island and Sharpsburg.

Only the words of people who experienced these mills firsthand can recreate what it was like to live in the presence of their epochal beauty and terror, and depend upon them for economic survival.

A sense of their loss became especially public and communal throughout the Steel Valley in 1988 when bulldozers demolished the Homestead Works—450 buildings connected by 150 miles of railroad tracks. The site of the mill, which covered an area as big as 330 football fields, is now an upscale commercial/industrial complex, a completely different scene for generations of townspeople strangely nurtured by the mill's noisy, gargantuan presence.

"My breathing dragon in the valley. What a sculpture! Why couldn't it have been sprayed for people to see?" Anna Marie Sninsky, 72, an artist, said to me in her studio where she once watched the Homestead plant in action. "The steam from the blast furnace formed plumes of white smoke that mingled with orange and red flames. It made a magnificent sight from the hills around here."

In *A Book About Myself* (1922), Theodore Dreiser describes seeing Pittsburgh for the first time in the 1890s: " . . . The whole river for a mile or more was suddenly lit to a rosy glow, a glow which, as I saw upon turning, came from the tops of some forty or fifty stacks belching an orange-red flame. At the same time an enormous pounding and crackling came from somewhere, as though Titans were at work upon subterranean anvils."

In this book I go beyond dramatic descriptions of the steel mills to show what life was like for the men inside and how it was for their wives and children at home. The leap is from romance to realism, the balance shifting with individual perspective, experience and memory. I try to capture the color, taste, sweat and wisdom of men and women toiling together. I especially try to rescue the stories of housewives that have never before been told. Because so much of the nation's past is preserved in terms of movements, trends and cycles, I have concentrated on individual lives and on what particular people say about working in the mills, living in a mill town, and growing up in a mill family in the years long before the mills closed.

Because we are all immigrants to this country, to honor the past of any is to strengthen us all. For in the alchemy of private and public memory is a mysterious and restorative grace.

Part I:
The Men in the Mills

Chapter 1

⚜️

Danger and Death

Frank's not goin' to come home.

The reality of a steel mill defies self-deception. Rats as big as dogs roamed the floors, especially on the riverside where they swam through the sewers like ancient water monsters. Brave souls picked them up by the tails and threw them into the molten iron. "It was dangerous and depressing to go into a large building with a thousand other guys—like going to prison and being trapped," William Pegler, an ex-steelworker, said in an unpublished interview for the Rivers of Steel National Heritage Area.

A genuine comfort level was impossible, steelworkers told me. Even though the buildings were barricaded behind high brick walls and barbed wire, their sides were open, making temperatures extremely hot in the summer and bitterly cold in the winter from rushing winds. Showers and locker rooms were rare before World War II. Men changed clothes behind their furnaces, the most dangerous and hottest place in any mill. They washed with river water that ran directly into metal tubs: "And it was dirty river water," one old-timer from the Edgar Thomson Works explains. "You'd break the ice, throw water on your face. The conditions was bad. But nobody said nothin'. Nobody complained."

The production floor was so hot that men covered it with wooden planks in order to walk. The planks often caught fire, burning their feet and creating more smoke to inhale. Before security clothes were required, workers tied handkerchiefs around their heads to absorb perspiration and wore long underwear in all seasons to smother flying sparks and prevent burns. Wives covered the holes with homemade patches.

"My father worked in the mill . . . and it's dirty, filthy hard work. World War II had terrible working conditions. Post-1960s workers romanticize it," Jerry Manning said in an oral history for the Rivers of Steel National Heritage Area.

Until World War II, steelworkers were almost entirely at the mercy of the owners in terms of safety, wages, and even survival. The story of men's lives in the Steel Valley is largely one of attempting to gain some power over their working conditions through unionization and through struggles with competing ethnic groups. Relationships in the mills were largely hierarchal, determined by job description and ethnicity.

Even the beloved mythic figure of Joe Magarac—strong enough to bend iron bars and stir molten steel with his bare hands—is a reflection of someone else's power, for the word *magarac* means *jackass* in Croatian. Magarac is the creation of Slavic immigrants who came to work in Pittsburgh steel plants in the late 1800s, but in naming their legendary character they absorbed how others defined them and mocked their own hard labor. "Not only Croatians but all Slavs were supposed to be jackasses in the mill—magaracs," said Steve Zoretich, a retired steelworker, born in 1903, in an interview for *Southwestern Pennsylvania* in 1983.

No matter the decade, the backbreaking work, heat and isolation of the mill were inescapable. A steelworker for thirty-three years, Martin Conners, 55, describes the massive anonymity of a mill in language as existential as one can imagine. For the world outside, the mill created a cinematic sky, but inside "it was like black and white television. Everything was covered with dull ash, and everything leaked. Especially in the wintertime, there'd be steam leaks all over the place, but you couldn't shut down because production would stop or it would freeze up. One time I was walking along and this butterfly came. A red butterfly. A monarch butterfly. That was the only color against this stark background. I heard that God was telling me, 'it's not so bad, Marty.' I was really down because I had lost my easy office job and was back where I started with a shovel, and here comes this butterfly. It really stood out."

In some cases, poetry captures the searing heat of molten iron and slag. A Homestead native and noted poet, Robert Gibb was a steelworker in his late twenties, during college and before Vietnam. "In the summertime you could be twenty feet from an oven, but it was like you had a candle flame up against your lips. You could feel it radiating against you. It was awful breathing all that dirt and dust for eight hours."

Gibb felt the heat of the mill in every pore of his body, but didn't realize it was also firing his imagination. Ten years after leaving the mill, Gibb wrote, "Entering the Oven," a poem in his prize-winning collection *The Origins of Evening*, which reads in part:

> Tonight, as usual,
> > evening's flared
> Like a slag heap down the rim
> Of the sky,
> > mills cast their sunsets
> On the waters, and we are entering
> The oven,
> > tearing a wall of fire-
> Bricks out of number 4's 120° depths.
> As long as we can bear it,
> > we hurl
> Crowbars at a wall blank as the face
> Of a whale,
> > rush back out for salt

And water, to put out our feet,
And sit clothed
                    by something other
Than flames. Cooled off, we reenter
That kingdom of heat
                    where the soles
Of our shoes start to smoulder,
Shirts flower with holes
                    like small,
Dark stars . . . until, finally, we are
Walking on fire
                    as if born to it, [. . .]

Gibb's description is viscerally and visually horrifying, but the most horrific experience for any steelworker to witness is the death or maiming of a peer. A retired couple, Jim and Rose Boland, recall injuries and accidents from years ago. Meeting them in their scaled-down apartment crammed with Notre Dame paraphernalia (including leprechauns and shamrocks in September), it's hard to imagine Jim without a 50-inch waistline and a stomach tucked under a very high belt, back when he pitched ore. But he did that for forty years and he loved working at an open hearth at Edgar Thomson, "the most dangerous place in the mill. I seen quite a few guys killed in there right alongside of us. The heat, you know. The slag. You're tapping two hundred tons of steel. A furnace would blow up or slag over-erupt," Jim tells me.

"One hot stinking morning," Jim remembers, "a worker was up on top of an overhead crane, inspecting it. Then someone moved the crane, and he was pinned between the crane and the overhead rail. There was no place to go and he was crushed to death. They got the painters up and painted right over the blood because the cranes was yellow. Nothing ever stopped. You know what I mean?" Jim asks.

Jim himself was spared from death at 3:20 in the afternoon on a day in a year that he and Rose can't quite pinpoint, but he remembers having looked at the clock. A civility between workers was to arrive early for a shift so that the man being relieved could get a head start for home. Jim was about to shovel out a furnace when his friend, "Old Dallas," arrived and said he'd take care of it so that Jim could get ready to leave. Walking off the floor, Jim turned around to see slag spilling out of control and Dallas burning. "Oh, God. He lived a few weeks. I went to the hospital to see him, but a nurse said you don't want to go in there."

When safety clothes and devices were required for workers after World War II, wearing prescription goggles and hard hats was a "pain" for Jim. "If you were an old-timer you just didn't want to listen to that crap," Jim points to his serge trousers and cotton shirt, explaining, "you went to work like this here, you might say. You only had to wear long underwear. And I liked it that way."

Jim once had slag slide down the back of his shoe and could hardly walk, but still went to work, Rose remembers. "I was the first one they ever packed in ice,"

Jim chimes in. He claims the plant physician learned from *Ben Casey*, the popular television series during the '50s, to treat burns with ice. "He packed my foot in ice, and after he saw that it worked, the mill always carried lots of ice," Jim says smugly.

Steelworkers are often connected to each other through violence, sometimes without even knowing each other's name. Charles Stewart was eighteen, working as a laborer at Edgar Thomson when he saw "a guy lose his hand in some gears. Oh, God. That memory will always be with me."

For a while Stewart thought it was exciting "to be around all that hot stuff, especially when walking on top of it, it burned your legs. For a kid, the mill was an exciting place to be. But it was risky. You could be killed."

After he served in World War II, Stewart found that the romance of the mill had faded, and he used the GI Bill to study commercial interior design.

But older steelworkers with families saw no way to leave the mill, even when they were scared. Ted Haas left his young family behind in New Castle, Pennsylvania, to take a job at the Irvin Works, a new plant for the Steel Valley, dedicated in 1938. He wrote a letter to his wife almost every night from November 1938 to May 1939, on stationery from the Clinton Hotel, in McKeesport, where he lived until he had enough money to send for her and the kids and buy a house. He was lonely, cold, hungry, fearful, courageous and dead honest. Through every emotion, his style is restrained. His letters were intended for his wife Ruth's eyes only, until his daughter, Sandy Doby, shared them with me.

On January 19, 1939, he reassures Ruth:

" . . . everything will turn out all right. I want a letter pretty quick I'm kinda lonesome I sleep a lot to forget but I can't help thinking when I'm awake. Well I'm still Feeder No 1. I don't know for how long   Machinery is going up pretty rapidly so I'm expecting a better job yet, so lets wait till it happens. You know when I came in this department there wasn't a bit of machinery. Now everything is up   There were 2 men that died. One died from heat failure   The other got killed in the Hot Strip   He's from New Castle. His name is Walter Baker. The Hot Strip is next door to us the very next department. The Fellow died 15 minutes after we took him to the hospital about 6:30 this morning. I think the company can make tin plate cheaper than kill their men off [That's] what it is to hurry the men up [They] want production and they don't care how they get it. Something will have to be done about it or the men will quit their jobs. All of them is scared of their jobs. I hope I keep up like I have been doing for I try to keep cool. I don't get excited about nothing. The hell with them and their production. I want to live a while yet."

Haas was powerless to change the condition of the mill, but he's a credible chronicler.

From the beginning until the end, the mills were never free from grisly accidents, death and suicide. At Chioda's, a blue-collar bar recently demolished after decades as a Homestead landmark, a retired steelworker nursed an Iron City, while yellowing bras of every size and shape swayed from the ceiling. He told me about his shock at finding the body of a co-worker hanging from a crane in the lonely hours of the midnight shift at the Homestead Works, hopeless about his future after the plant closed.

Mike Stout was the top grievance representative for the Steelworkers Union when Homestead closed in 1986. He's still edgy. Meeting with him at the Steel Valley Printers, a shop he owns on Homestead's Eighth Avenue, was like entering a set for a film noir. Gaining his full attention wasn't easy until I described my grandfather's death back in 1907. Then he told me about seeing men hurt in the mill "all the time. Saw a guy get his toes cut off. Saw another guy catch his face on the edge of a slab and cut his entire face open. If we didn't keep him awake, he would have died right on the spot. . . . That's pretty much the story of just about everybody here. They've been shortchanged." Stout looks around his shop, taking in the displaced steelworkers he employs and the Homestead history buffs who hang out there.

Shortly after leaving Steel Valley Printers, I went to a nursing home to visit with Mary Koltin, 89, because I wanted to hear firsthand how wives learned about death in the kind of accidents I had heard about. She relived the day, fifty-five years ago, when her husband Frank, then 34, was critically injured.

She was spending a typical Sunday afternoon, preparing dinner with her mother and sister, while Frank worked the 8 to 4 shift. When he wasn't home by five o'clock, she looked out the window to see a car pull up to the curb and two men beckon her father on his way back from playing cards at one of the Steel Valley's nationality clubs. "My dad just reeled up the driveway, and I said to my mother, 'is he drunk?' But he was in shock and just says to me, 'Frank's not goin' to come home.'"

The hospital wouldn't release any details to Mary until she was officially notified by the steel company. But that never happened. "In a few hours, the fellow who was head of maintenance came over and then a friend drove me to the emergency room."

Through hard tears but without self-pity, Mary is precise. A 3,500-pound furnace door fell on Frank, catching him from the waist down, crushing his bones and ripping his kidneys, as he tried to run away from it. Men on the previous shift had not attached the hinges properly. "Two fellows seen it and knew it was wrong, but wouldn't go as witnesses because they had kids too and would have lost their jobs," Mary says with the understanding only a mill wife could muster. Frank lived for three days, and told Mary he'd work for 25 cents an hour rather than go back to the same job as a burner in the mill.

Mary didn't receive a penny of compensation but was offered a job as a janitor in the mill, where she worked for twenty-four years, cleaning five floors of bathrooms at the Homestead Works, earning $2.00 an hour to support two children under the age of five (eventually her hourly pay rose to $6.00).

"I had to get up to be at work at seven. And I'd get my stuff all ready and go from floor to floor, to do the mirrors, do the sinks, do the toilets, do the floors." But Mary enjoyed the camaraderie of the mill. "One girl said to me, 'hey, Koltin, do you want a party when you retire?' I says, 'I don't want no party. Just give me the money. I ain't goin' out there to get drunk with yunz.' So I got $500 and a beautiful spread and drapes to match."

When steelworkers, like Mary's husband, were critically injured or killed while on the job, the family was not allowed to see where the tragedy had occurred. Jim Boland remembers seeing "priests coming in for last rites, and the coroner, but nobody else. If it had happened to me, Rose couldn't run down and go in that mill. That was a policy," he adds reverentially.

One retired steelworker still regrets following orders for a cleanup, bringing things up to safety code, after a load of steel collapsed. Twenty years later, he sets the scene for me.

The heavy chain looping around sheets of finished steel had slipped off, causing tons of steel to fall like a deck of cards on a worker during the four to midnight shift.

"He looked okay until they took off his belt in the infirmary, and his guts came out. On the midnight to eight shift, we had to clean everything up because there was going to be an investigation the next day, and the place was really unsafe. We painted safety lines where they were supposed to be, and made everything neat and spiffy. I thought, 'They're trying to make it look good to put the shaft to the poor widow. Trying to make it look like his fault.' And I didn't want to be part of making this place look good. I kept thinking about the wife being screwed out of her insurance."

When a tragic accident occurred, steelworkers didn't talk much about it, Earl Birdy, 68, told me, as we sat in the den of his suburban home, surrounded by blown-up pictures of his days as a referee for Pitt football games. Nearly fifty years ago, he saw a coworker "cooked to death" in an asbestos safety suit when a breakout occurred in the wall of a furnace as he was tapping out a heat. "A crane operator put a hook over him, but the guy's arms were so scalded he couldn't hold on. I don't remember his last name—only Augie—but it was the turning point in my life. I'm not sure I ever told my kids about it, but right then I knew I had to go to college, no matter what my dad thought. The mill was just too dangerous."

Because of the union, skilled workers during the '60s and '70s earned higher salaries than many professionals, making it hard for steelworkers like Birdy's father to understand why their sons would want to go to college. Getting a job in a steel plant, not a seat in a freshman class, was therefore the main goal of most boys of steelworking families. "All the fellows I grew up with planned to work in the mills like their fathers, uncle and brothers. That's all they knew," said Mary Ann Boytim, a mill wife, in an interview with the Rivers of Steel National Heritage Area. "'I want to do man's work.' How many times did I hear that during high school," Dan Karaczun, a Duquesne University graduate said in a similar interview. "That meant using your hands and your back, not your brain, to make a living."

George De Bolt, a lifetime resident of Homestead, attended a local elementary school, but then transferred to an independent school in the sixth grade after a top administrator in the Homestead-Munhall school district told his parents "'quite honestly, we're educating kids to be steelworkers.'"

The librarian at Munhall High School, Mary Howat, now 88, tried persuading seniors to read *Out of This Furnace*, Thomas Bell's classic novel about the lives of early steelworkers in southwestern Pennsylvania, "but they'd say, 'soon we'll be making more money than you.'"

"The mill was a good place to make money," agrees Dan Koltin, Frank and Mary Koltin's son, who became a Spanish teacher at Steel Valley High School. "Kids would say to me, 'I'm goin' down the mill. Don't have to know anything you're teachin'.'" Koltin always advised boys with this attitude to learn a skilled trade. "Be a plumber, electrician, carpenter, something. Just don't walk into the mill, expecting a good job." A student once asked Koltin his salary. "In 1972, I was not even making $7,500 a year. Then the kid says, 'I'll be making $25,000 down the mill.' The mill was a good living, but I guess I just had enough sense to say, 'hey, I don't want that kind of life.'"

But kids had to have "whiskers" before earning high salaries as steelworkers, and most had little understanding of the years it could take to get them. Martin Conners, a retired mill veteran, started in the labor department of LTV Steel at $2.35 an hour in September 1966. "When you first go in the mill, you got the dirty jobs because people said you didn't have enough whiskers. You didn't have the seniority. When I finally got my whiskers, and my turn at bat, that's when they shut the place down."

Kids always got hard jobs, standing in grease pits, shoveling them out by hand, while wearing boots and suits that made them sweat. "They always said it was easier on the young guys," says Conners. "But I never found it easier. I never did. I came into the mill a young man and left an old one."

Extreme temperatures in the mill and strenuous labor took their toll, and the schedule was brutal because of the way shifts were set up. The shifts were generally from 8 A.M. to 4 P.M., 4 P.M. to midnight, and midnight to 8 A.M. During the '60s and '70s, men sometimes worked three daylight turns with forty-eight hours off, before returning for two midnight shifts, all in one week. More typically, a worker had the same shift for a week.

Either way, by the time a worker adjusted to a shift, it was over. When he worked the three shifts, his days off changed. One week, he might be free on Wednesday and Thursday; the next week, on Tuesday. "Working shifts was horrible," says Mike Stout. "You didn't have a life. You had to sleep and eat at different hours every week. It threw your whole body out of kilter."

Unlike the blue-collar workers, office personnel worked steady daylight turns. The differences between the schedules consistently created tension. "We did all the hard work and they got all the benefits," is Conner's perception. "They were in air conditioning in the summer and had heat in the winter. They got to wear clean clothes plus they had weekends and holidays off. We had to work whatever turn came up, even if it was 8 to 4 on Christmas Day."

Robert Gibb had an epiphany about a steelworker's life one morning as he was leaving the midnight shift and spotted the "guy in charge of my labor gang—called a pusher"—buying donuts in a local bakery. Without his safety hat, the pusher was clearly a balding old man. "It clicked with me that he had spent his whole life down there in the mill, and I knew that's not what I wanted to do. I began to understand the condition of the lives around me, and what it would be like to do stuff like that my whole life. Growing up, you think that's the way things are and you sleepwalk through them."

Later, in the poem "Entering the Oven," Gibb captures, without nostalgia, the ceremonial bonds which have always connected steelworkers: "Night after night the man with / The white hat / and all the pens / Calls out names and accidents from / The preceding shifts. . . ."

The man with the white hat was a boss. The bosses in the mills wore white safety hats to separate them from the workers, who wore orange hats. But unlike the cowboys in Western films, the white hats represented the bad guys.

Negative images of white hats are burned into the psyches of steelworkers of every generation. "They were the wage slaves . . . lord and master," Raymond Stevens, 86, fumed like a fifteen-year-old water boy, as he sat with me at a meeting of retired union steelworkers at the Homestead Elks. "Had a relative who never drank until he went into supervision. Kidneys went from drinking."

Even when white hats had been promoted through the mill system, the perception was that they quickly forgot those they left behind. "It's like the army," one man said to me. "Whenever somebody's a private or corporal and is promoted to sergeant, he forgets all about being a private."

Martin Conners' father-in-law was a boss in the mill. "We got along okay," says Conners, "but he was always a white hat to me, a company man. They didn't have a union to back them up, so they had to toe the company line."

The tyranny of steel bosses was an enduring threat to workers, no matter the decade. For example, Joe Payne creates a mythic figure in his description of John Huey, a white hat from the '40s. Showing the vitality of an artist with an appetite for character, setting and magic, Payne described Huey in an oral history for the Rivers of Steel National Heritage Area.

> "Every time John came through the slab mill, which was very, very hot, you could feel the wind go by, that's how cold he was. One day, the good Lord took care of him, and he fell over. His men picked him up, put him in an ambulance, took him to West Penn Hospital. A month later, back to work, he walks through the same yard. [You] can still feel the breeze going by, and he never said hello to them, nothing. Fellas said, 'what kinda man is he?'
>
> Six months later, goes through the yard again, falls [out] a second time—equilibrium. Some men picked him up, ambulance, hospital. Out six months this time. Back to work, same thing, didn't speak to nobody."

By this time, Joe, a grievance officer, had dealt with a case against John Huey and got him off. After that happened a second time, Joe felt comfortable about walking into Huey's office. He was smoking a cigar, shoes off, and feet on the desk.

Joe never heard a man "speak so politely," and figured Huey was in a very good mood. "So he says, 'John, let me ask you a question. I'm not working for you right now. I'm working for the union.'

John says, 'What's your question?' And I hit him. 'Are you a human bein' or what are you?'

He asks, 'What do you mean?'

'Those guys picked you up twice, and you came back to work and didn't even look at 'em.'

He said, 'When that mill goes down, Joe [when production is stopped for some reason] who blows that whistle? I do. When I blow that whistle, my boss up the general office hears that. Then my phone rings [and] he says, 'What's goin' on down there, and how long will it take to fix it?'

'I have a quarter mile to walk to see what's wrong. But I don't even know what's wrong yet,' he says. 'So when I walk through that mill, I don't see those men. I see that devil up there. My boss.'

The next year, Huey retired and Joe was called for jury duty. "And who do you think is on jury duty? Him. He grabbed me and put his arms around me. Wanted to buy me dinner. Changed man. That's what the hell the company does to their own people."

"You saw *The Deerhunter*?" asks Bob Qualters, whose paintings of the Steel Valley hang in museums, galleries and corporate offices. "Those guys were not prototypical steelworkers at all. It's a wonderful movie but De Niro and Walken were larger than life. Much more heroic and dashing. Most of the steelworkers I knew were pretty ordinary people. They wanted their cabins and motorboats. They wanted to get out of those houses in West Mifflin, get a boat, get married and have kids." For years, the most requested vacation day in the mills was the first Monday after Thanksgiving, the opening of deer hunting season.

To buy their boats, cabins and hunting rifles, steelworkers tolerated stubborn white hats and accepted as part of life the tension between labor, management and government. But above all, they believed that Big Steel would always be there for them, eternal, accepting, inventive, forgiving and paternal.

"What the company gives you, it can take right back," Bill O'Leary warned early in 1937 when Carnegie-Illinois suddenly recognized the Steel Workers Organizing Committee (SWOC), granting a five-day week and an eight-hour day.

"What the company gives you, it can take right back," was the mantra in the mills for decades, said by rote, without belief, until the moment that they actually closed.

Chapter 2

⋘⁂⋙

Steelworkers Find a Voice
Anyone trying to organize workers would be fired.

Bloody disputes about hours, wages and safety defined steelworkers' lives from the very beginning of the industry. The Homestead Lockout and Strike of 1892 and the Great Steel Strike of 1919, known as the Hunky Strike, are fresh and personal to many in the Steel Valley whose names will never compete with Andrew Carnegie or Henry Clay Frick. Yet it is the Brozeks, Beleveks, Shatlocks and De Bolts who expose the direct clash between the power world of the steel industry and the very vulnerable, human one of the workers. Their words and images bring us into the presence of America's industrial past. They describe secret meetings of unionizers, childhood memories of Iron and Steel Police, fathers working twelve-hour days and seven-day weeks, and efforts of Big Steel to thwart ethnic solidarity. They reveal life inside the mills as a contradiction of personal connection and betrayal, a ladder of hierarchal relationships, social oppression and ethnic and racial tension.

George De Bolt, 56, is the only descendent of a Homestead Strike leader still living in Homestead. His grandfather, George Solomon De Bolt, was one of 33 union organizers arrested for murder and treason, but the charges were dropped after juries in the first three trials acquitted the defendants. Another 170 strikers were arrested on charges of murder and inciting a riot.

George and I talked about his grandfather in Chioda's Tavern, a Homestead landmark, "world renowned . . . established in 1895." After ordering from a plastic menu listing jalapeño bombs, pierogies, haluski, and "mother's Wednesday night spaghetti special," we settled into our conversation, surrounded by yellowing maps of the Monongahela River, aerial shots of the mills, glossies of dead Pittsburgh boxers, and lots of cigarette smoke.

"The uprising occurred in July, but folks were being arrested in September and October in order to set an example," said De Bolt, president of the Homestead and Mifflin Township Historical Society. "They were going to teach those rabble-rousers a lesson. Word got around, and they were all finally blacklisted and couldn't work in any steel plant."

The crisis began when the Amalgamated Association of Iron and Steel Workers was negotiating a new contract for skilled laborers at the Carnegie Steel Company, later the Homestead Works. Henry Clay Frick, Carnegie's associate, countered with an offer that would reduce their wages. If the union would not accept the new terms and respond by June 24, the Company threatened to bargain only with individual workers. Frick further angered the workers by constructing a ten-foot-high fence, topped with barbed wire and electric searchlights, around the mill.

Negotiations broke down on June 23 when Frick did not accept the union's proposal and declared the mill permanently nonunionized. The rebellion itself began when the Company locked out the entire workforce of 3,800 on the morning of June 30. Frick's terms affected 325 union men, but at the lockout and over the summer, 3,000 more workers joined them in protest.

Frick hired the Pinkerton National Detective Agency in New York to send 300 agents from there and Chicago to protect the plant while strikebreakers continued production. Early on the morning of July 6, two barges carrying Pinkerton guards attempted to land on the banks of the Monongahela River near the mill. Hundreds of town residents—men, women and children—were ready for them with oil, gunpowder and dynamite. Gunshots were exchanged and a barge was set on fire. The bloody riot lasted for thirteen hours, from 4 A.M. to 5 P.M., when the Pinkertons surrendered to the steelworkers. Three Pinkertons and seven Homestead residents had been killed, and many had been wounded.

After holding the "Pinks" for twenty-four hours, the townspeople marched them ignominiously through the crowds before allowing them to leave. Within a few days, at Frick's request, Governor Robert Pattison dispatched 8,500 State Militia. They controlled Homestead for five months. The strike ended on November 17, when some workers returned to the plant and some new ones were hired. All of them, according to Peter Krass in his book *Carnegie*, had to "sign a pledge of loyalty and a statement declaring that [they] had not been on company grounds, had not participated in the rioting, and did not know anyone who did." Management had effectively broken labor's back. The union was driven out for forty years, and Homestead became known as a "company town."

Surprising me, George said he hadn't grown up listening to stories about his grandfather's role in the strike. "It wasn't the sort of thing you talked about. Remember, my grandfather was put into jail, so that wasn't anything to be very proud of. Back then, you were taught to be ashamed of your involvement in the strike. After the battle Carnegie Steel basically said the only people who're going to work in the mill are those who will renounce the union. There was also a great feeling here that the steel plant had spies and anyone trying to organize workers again would be fired. Things were so bad for the leaders of the union that they left Homestead. People didn't want to be associated with them."

That's why De Bolt knows he is the only direct descendent of a union organizer still living in the town.

As a student at Wesleyan University, De Bolt began to see his grandfather as a very brave man. "It was the sensibility of the '60s to value involvement in a cause as something to be proud of, and to admire individuals who stood up for their community. A whole generation believed we could make the world a better place. But just think of the mentality of 1892," De Bolt revs up, forgetting to eat. "The man was arrested for treason. He can't get a job, and nobody wants to be his friend for fear of being tainted. But in my mind now, there's no question he's a hero."

De Bolt's grandfather stayed in Homestead because his young wife gave birth to a boy a few days after the lockout. The only job he could get was mucking out stables, which made him aware of an immediate need for bulk delivery of feed, grain and hay. By 1895, he had saved enough money to buy a horse and wagon, and in 1914, he bought his first truck, which was the beginning of a lucrative family business in truck and bus transportation that George now runs.

When George was a little boy, De Bolt trucks hauled material in and out of the steelmills that had blacklisted his grandfather. George's father, John Pierpont Morgan De Bolt—who had no name for months while his parents debated one befitting a future captain of commerce—delighted in smuggling young George into the mills, hidden under tarps or squashed under a seat. "Dad knew all the foremen and cranemen, so once I got past the dispatcher I could get out of the truck and see how steel was made."

As a teenager working beside his father, George finally entered the mill legitimately. "That was a real treat for me," he adds, "because the mill was an amazing place and none of my peers could get in without a superintendent signing off."

After graduation from Wesleyan and service in the Peace Corps, De Bolt couldn't wait to get back to Homestead. "My father loved this town, with all the stuff that comes with it, and so do I," he says. Using as a metaphor the high fences that once surrounded the steel plant, De Bolt refers to Homestead as a "walled city," difficult to penetrate with new ideas. He thinks that's part of the legacy of the 1892 strike. "It's a town that's suspicious of big business, of capital, because the relationship between management and labor has always been so confrontational here. People complained about U. S. Steel meddling in their lives, but when the town wanted anything, the company made donations and helped to make it happen. Planning for the future, thinking about the future was something you didn't need to do while the mills were here. Workers wanted their kids' lives to be better than theirs and to have the kids go to college, but if they got a job in the mill, that was okay, too, because your dad worked in the mill and did well. The mills essentially took care of people."

Such benevolent memories of Big Steel make it difficult for many Homestead residents to accept The Waterfront, a $300-million upscale retail, entertainment, office and residential complex, now occupying the space where the Works stood. For example, Eugene Shatlock, 81, one of the oldest mill kids I talked with, was born in the same house where his grandfather lived during the Homestead Strike, smack up against the steel plant where TGIFriday's is now. "When we have dinner there, I can't believe where I am. My father and grandfather would turn over in their graves if they could see what's happened here."

But miles from The Waterfront, Eugene and his wife Isabel graciously welcomed me into their meticulously kept suburban home where sunlight filtered through sheer curtains and danced across Havilland figurines, a fragile setting for a conversation about a bloody riot. Eugene's grandfather and George Solomon De Bolt, it turned out, experienced the Homestead Strike from different perspectives.

Martin Schattlack had been an equestrian for Kaiser Wilhelm I of Germany, grooming his horses and driving his carriage during the 1870s. He came to the United States in 1880, directly to the Pittsburgh Bessemer Steel Company in Homestead, two years before Andrew Carnegie purchased it, because he had heard that the mill depended upon horses for transportation. An impatient clerk in the hiring office shortened the spelling of his name to Shatlock, Eugene told me.

Martin was not a union member, but he patrolled the mill gate in solidarity with union and nonunion workers to prevent scabs from entering. When Frick's fence went up, his fears increased about his wife and children living only a half block away from the scene of the action.

On the morning of July 6, 1892, when fighting began, Martin and a son, both unarmed, watched from a hill and returned home when gunfire rang out. The family listened and remained cloistered until news came of the Pinkertons' surrender. During the five months of militia occupation, the family felt under house arrest, and Martin continued to worry about their safety. Guardsmen were always lurking because the mill was virtually in the Shatlocks' backyard.

Between July 14 and September 16, 1892, George Reynolds, a member of the militia, wrote letters to Elizabeth Jones, his sweetheart, in Oil City, Pennsylvania. The authentic voice of a guardsman is seldom heard in the labor histories of the Homestead Strike. These unpublished letters are a reliable account of an ordinary young man trying to describe the danger of his situation without causing alarm.

"From Homestead, Wednesday, July 28th," Reynolds writes:

Dear Lizzie,
. . . The boys [the Second Brigade Band] are all tired out for they did not get any sleep   they had to keep moving around last night more than ever because they were making some arrests and the strikers would gather around in crowds and the boys had to disperse the crowd as soon as they could [. . . .] I went over through the mill. There is more machinery in one of their buildings than you could put in all of the Pipe Line shops and they have some buildings just as large as that so you can make up your mind that it is a big mill [. . . .] There are about seven hundred scabs working there now. [They] eat sleep and work all in the same building for they are afraid to show their face out of the mill for fear they get shot full of holes. The strikers are just beginning to realise that they are being driven out and away from home and work. I tell you Lizzie it does look tough for Old Frick has ordered them to leave the company houses in ten days or the Sherriffe and Guards will have to throw them out. [D]oes it not look tough[?] The men that are there now are mostly polocks huns [sic] and Italians. They bring them in on boats from Pittsburgh   dare not bring them in on train. . . .

He describes trips to Pittsburgh to see the Exposition, and walking to Swissvale and Braddock to catch a baseball game or buy tobacco. Returning to Homestead, he again feels threatened. He refers to guardmen being called to settle a mill skirmish in Duquesne on August 4: "We are just starting for the Ducane [*sic*] Iron Mill. They are having some trouble up there and the 16 was ordered out but I guess all will be quiet when we get there. It is 8 miles up the River." Reynolds worries that the militia will be in Homestead throughout the winter, but the strike ends in November, allowing him to return to Lizzie.

The day before the strike ended on November 20, when the workers essentially gave up, the *Homestead Local News* reported: "For a month or more it has been apparent that the workmen could not win and a prolongation of the strike was simply a useless sacrifice." About three hundred "Hungarian and Slav workmen, were the first to break away . . . and half the number were given employment at once and the remainder were promised work sooner or later. This break was the forerunner of a larger and more important one yesterday afternoon, which included the English speaking laborers and the mechanincs . . . with a limited number of the Amalgamated men."

The language of the report clearly reveals the hierarchy of mill jobs based on ethnic identity, and the resignation of people expecting more of the same. In 1892, the population of Homestead was 12,000, having attracted Irish, Scottish and German immigrants in the early 1880s, who held highly skilled jobs in the mill. Later immigrants from Russia, Italy, Poland and Eastern Europe had unskilled jobs. The cycle would continue with the newest wave of immigrant workers, most of them from Eastern Europe, locked into the lowest paying jobs, with little hope for advancement.

As a nonunion skilled worker, Martin Shatlock returned to his former job hauling light material within the plant by horseback. After twenty-eight years of service, he retired from the transportation department in 1909, with a monthly pension of $10, which he supplemented by sweeping the streets of Homestead until his death at the age of eighty-four.

Looking like the owner of a pineapple plantation in his starched white embroidered shirt, Eugene has a history at odds with his *persona,* but in sync with his grandfather's legacy. Eugene was the first Shatlock to become a union member. Hired in 1940 as a laborer in the Homestead Works, he was required to join the United Steelworkers' Union. He was exempt from the military because of doing essential work in the armor plate machine shop where steel was made for the gun turrets on battleships. But without telling his parents, he enlisted in the Navy and served in the South Pacific. On the GI Bill, Eugene graduated from Dartmouth in 1946 and completed an MBA at the University of Pittsburgh. He retired in 1983 as an executive in the treasury department of U. S. Steel, a position his grandfather would never have imagined for himself while protecting "Fort Frick" against the strikebreakers.

Liz Mowry, 67, a second-generation mill kid, heard about my research and called me about her paternal grandfather, John Joseph Handschuh, hired at Carnegie Steel five years before the strike, and retired in 1921.

Her home was in holiday transition. Porcelain Halloween pumpkins sitting beside a Christmas crèche and bedraggled straw turkey gave the appearance of disorganized clutter, until I saw row upon row of three-ring binders neatly documenting years of precious family history with obituaries, recipes, newspaper clippings, rent receipts, diaries, letters and genealogy charts beginning when sixteen-year-old Handschuh left Waserolerving, Germany in 1872.

Describing him as the "right-hand man to Andrew Carnegie," Liz showed me a picture of her grandfather with two other men, taken in 1887, and turned over to her by U. S. Steel one hundred years later, when it was found pasted to an old wall safe. " . . . the three men that helped to roll the first steel armor plate in Homestead, Pa., Allegheny County, December the 24th, 1887," reads the original note on the back.

Liz was a child when her grandfather died in 1944, but family lore is that Carnegie often visited his home. Obituaries in local papers refer to him as "a friend of the late Andrew Carnegie and C. M. Schwab, the steel 'giants' of their day." Another obituary says he "rubbed shoulders" with them. Liz's own father often talked about his father's association with Carnegie, but Liz "never thought too much about it until later in life." No doubt Handschuh was popular. The guest book from his funeral has hundreds of signatures; "everybody that was anybody in Homestead was there," Liz interprets.

But Liz has no idea what part Handschuh played in the Homestead Strike; in fact, no one in her family does. "There's no documentation that he was working against the workers," Liz offers, and then says aloud, as if admitting for the first time: "You know, I think that's something that the family didn't want to ever find out about. You know what I mean? . . . But if there were [documentation] they probably wouldn't want to know that. Because they all worked there."

Among all her scrapbooks, receipts, pictures and artifacts, Liz has no final word on her grandfather's role in the Homestead Strike of 1892. Talking about the strike more than a century later, is still tricky business in Homestead.

When the strike ended, the workers who were not blacklisted and chose to return to the mill had lower wages and generally worked twelve-hour days, seven-day weeks. Bill Belevek, 89, a mill kid and retired steelworker, brought me closer to those years by describing 1919, a significant year in labor history because the Great Steel Strike—or the Hunky Strike—that began on September 27 was the largest walkout until then in steel history.

"I must have been about six," he says, pushing back his baseball cap to think better. "Hot metal seeped out of the hatch and burned a part of my dad's leg off. He was handicapped all his life. But they didn't have the coverage we have today, you understand, workmen's comp or whatever. . . . We were in poverty way before the Depression. It started with Calvin Coolidge right through Herbert Hoover."

I talked with Bill Belevek at the Rankin Boro building where he works as a volunteer by answering the phone, close to the four-room house where he grew up with nine siblings. His parents married in Yugoslavia and came directly to Rankin because Eastern Europeans were being hired in the mills. "We were dirt poor, but my mother was able to hold things together by sewing and cooking. She used to make a meal for us in a big pot that'd last for two days," Bill remembers. He imitates how a baker yelled out the window from his shop next to their house: "'Hey, Mrs. Belevek. You need more flour sacks?' She'd buy 'em for a nickel apiece, dye them blue and make the best damned shirts you ever wore. Something like your blue denim, only better."

As evidenced by the Belevek family, conditions for the steelworkers did not improve after the strike of 1892. Wages for all workers declined because they were set at "what the market could bear," instead of on a sliding scale which had benefited skilled workers and encouraged their production before the strike of 1892. For example, a roller in the mill averaged $11.09 per day in 1892 but $7.38 in 1907, according to John Fitch, an investigator of labor practices in the steel industry in Pittsburgh and author of *The Steel Workers*, a classic study published in 1910. And the typical work schedule increased to twelve-hour days and seven-day weeks for most departments in all Steel Valley plants.

"It's slavery and persecution. It's a prison. We work behind locked doors and can't leave the mill except for a few minutes at a certain time. . . . What kind of life is it to live here and see nothing but the mill, even when I don't work. . . . A man could live twice as long if he had the eight-hour day. This way one doesn't want to live long. What is the use of living, since one doesn't enjoy life? . . ," asks Mike Connolly, a worker in the Jones & Laughlin mill, in a 1920 interview kept in the archives of the Rivers of Steel National Heritage Area.

To talk about shorter hours, higher wages and safer working conditions, workers met in homes or nationality clubs, where informers could easily be spotted, and they often used women to carry messages between meetings because management's spies were less likely to be watching women. The steel companies squelched any attempt workers made to find a voice.

But labor leaders grew more optimistic during World War I when steelworkers were in a better position to make demands. Labor was scarce because 60,000 men from the Pittsburgh region had gone off to fight for the Allied cause. And yet "eighty percent of all munitions steel used by the United States Army came from the Pittsburgh mills," according to Frank Murdock in "Some Aspects of Pittsburgh's Industrial Contributions to the War, " a speech he gave before the Historical Society of Western Pennsylvania on May 31, 1921, based on information from the Ordinance Department of the city of Pittsburgh.

When the Armistice in 1918 halted the need for munitions, and the steel industry began trimming the labor force, Amalgamated feared losing the leverage it had gained during the war. The time seemed ripe for a more strategic, organized effort on behalf of labor, the union reasoned, and decided to join with other craft unions representing workers in various kinds of unskilled jobs under the umbrella of the American Federation of Labor (AFL). Within a year of the Armistice, preparations were in place for the Great Steel Strike.

The Great Steel Strike, or "Hunky Strike," that began on September 22, 1919, was the largest walkout until then in the steel industry, for some 365,000 workers in iron and steel mills in ten states and fifty cities left their jobs, bringing production to a halt. More than 32,000 workers in the Steel Valley participated. The strike ended on January 8, 1920, when "the National Committee for Organizing Iron and Steel Workers voted to permit the 100,000 or more men still on strike to return to work upon the best terms they could secure," according to William Z. Foster, one of the organizers and author of *The Great Steel Strike and Its Lessons.*

A major difference between the Homestead Strike of 1892 and The Hunky Strike of 1919 was that unskilled workers, largely Eastern Europeans, were in the majority in 1919. The steel industry used the term "Hunky Strike" to intimidate "American" workers into believing that by supporting the strike they could lose their jobs to the Eastern European "foreigners," who would then take over the steel industry. In fact, Foster laments that "American-born" men, once "bold, militant and tenacious as bulldogs" in the Homestead Strike, "had lost much of their independent spirit . . . [and] hesitate to put in jeopardy their comparatively good jobs. . . . "

The hunkies in the Great Strike of 1919 were the "new immigrants"—the Slavs, Hungarians, Bulgarians, Poles, Greeks and Italians—who were divided by language, culture and custom. The Scotch and Irish who had arrived in the 1860s and '70s, spoke English and had the best jobs in the mills. When they became bosses, they hired other Scots and Irish for the open-hearths and blast furnaces, where bonuses were often given for increased production, doubling a steelworker's straight pay. In *The Steel Workers,* Fitch notes "little tendency on the part of the foremen and superintendents to promote a Slav workman to the highest position even if he is fitted for it. . . . I was unable to learn of any Slav who had worked up to positions as roller or heaters [in 1907-08]. . . . It is the general impression among the mill-workers that a Slav will not be promoted so long as an English-speaking man is to be secured."

One Slav, Alex Kolson, was rescued by his young daughter Mary from working as a chipper, a job chopping rough edges from ingots to make them ready for the rolling mill. Mary Kolson's husband Charles Stewart told me the story in memory of her. As a little girl, Mary spoke only Slovak and lived in the Ward, the immigrant community in Homestead that was surrounded on three sides by the steel mill and on the fourth side by two railroad tracks. She walked to the Homestead Library every day for English lessons, and taught her father to speak English so that he could get a better job. "He was a mill hunky and they were never promoted," explains Stewart, "but he learned the language and eventually became a crane operator."

The Hunky Strike was driven by unskilled laborers like Alex Kolson who objected to working twelve-hour days and seven-day weeks, with little hope for advancement. In Braddock, the center of the strike, parents had walked their children to school but when the strike started in September, "Coal and Iron Police came along and just dispersed the crowds" in front of St. Michael's, a Slavic school and parish. "School or no school, kids or no kids. 'Cause you were only allowed three people to talk together. And the horses were so trained that if you got smart talking to the police, the horses would step on your feet," recalls Stan Brozek, a nine-year-old mill kid at the time, in an oral history he gave in 1992 for the Rivers of Steel National Heritage Area.

A lifelong resident of Braddock, Harry Lucas, born in 1923, remembers his mother describing the town's high level of fear. "Guards mounted on horses went straight up to the people's houses. . . . They beat 'em with clubs for no reason at all . . . and the Braddock police didn't do anything," he adds.

Stories are legion about the brutality of the Coal and Iron Police, the Pinkerton security force hired by the steel companies that had the authority of the Commonwealth to patrol the milltowns. Chuck Prezmonti, born in 1916, remembers his father talking about seeing "the Cossacks" following two men into a house and beating them. Prezmonti's dad "grabbed one off his horse and threw him down on the ground." The men were able to rally and beat off the guards, but they worried about being traced and run down again. Residents of Braddock and Homestead referred to the Coal and Iron Police as Cossacks, the constabulary they had fled in their Eastern European villages.

The living condition of millworking families in this fearful atmosphere was the major concern of Mary Heaton Vorse and Mother (Mary Harris) Jones. An investigative reporter and eyewitness to the strike of 1919, Vorse writes in *Men and Steel* (1920), now out of print: "All of Braddock is black. The soot of the mills has covered it. There is no spot in Braddock that is fair to see. It has neither park nor playground. Those who have made money in Braddock mills live where they cannot see Braddock. The steel [workers] who can[,]escape up the hillsides . . . but many of them live and die in the First Ward. . . . The decencies of life ebb away as one nears the mills. . . . No green thing grows anywhere. . . . Generation after generation of children, born where no green thing grows. . . . Power which can treat men's lives as commodities . . . , against this despotism the workers had revolted."

In her *Autobiography,* Mother Jones describes traveling "up and down the Monongahela River [visiting] the places where the steelworkers were on strike [and] meetings were forbidden. If I were to stop to talk to a woman on the street about her child, a Cossack would come charging down upon us and we would have to run for our lives. If I were to talk to a man in the streets of Braddock, we would be arrested for unlawful assembly." She was arrested in Homestead for trying to talk with workers at a public meeting.

Freedom of speech and assembly was a major hurdle for the strikers. Local authorities throughout the valley cooperated with the steel companies by denying applications for organizers to meet. When permits were granted, they usually stipulated that all public speakers use English, or risk being arrested. While most steelworkers spoke Slovak, some spoke Russian, Polish, Italian and Bulgarian.

The one safe meeting place in Braddock was the basement of St. Michael's Church, only a block away from the entrance to the Edgar Thomson Works. A recently placed marker acknowledges that "Rev. Adalbert Kazincy, pastor of St. Michael's championed the strikers." When the Coal and Iron Police tried to break up their meetings, Father Kazincy faced them down, saying, "This is a house of God, and you can't come in here." He spoke from the pulpit against economic injustice, and threatened to post a sign saying, "This church of Christ closed by the United States Steel Corporation," if attempts were made to intimidate him.

Largely because workers were separated by distance and because steel company authorities used physical force and intimidation, on January 8, 1920 the Hunky Strike ended with little immediate gain for the workers and little or no change in the engrained pattern of mill politics, conflict and culture that preceded the strike and led to the use of *hunky* in naming it.

Martin Conners, 55, amiable and affable during much of our conversation about his days as a steelworker, became red-faced talking about the Hunky Strike, although it happened long before he was born. "Every ethnic group had its slur, but the rottenest thing you could be called was a 'dumb hunky.' It was like calling a black person you know what, or using *dago*. . . . But the worst was 'dumb hunky' because that had broader meaning. 'Look at that dumb steelworker. That's all he can do. You're so dumb you couldn't get a better job.' That's what it implied."

For some, like Conners, *hunky* is a demeaning term for a person of Austrian-Hungarian heritage. "The Irish saw themselves as blue-blooded wasps, and called all Eastern Europeans hunkies, lumped them all together and felt superior," said a man with an Irish mother. Another woman remembers her Irish father, a laborer in the mill, raising her Austrian mother's blood pressure by calling her brothers, who were in management, hunkies.

But for many in the Steel Valley, "hunky" is a neutral word, embracing anybody working in a steel mill. "People talk about themselves as being mill hunkies but that doesn't mean they're Hungarian or it's a slur. It was just a part of who you were and how you described yourself," explains Bonnie Harvey, CEO of the Carnegie Library in Homestead, a mill kid, whose own heritage is Irish, Scottish and German.

Her paternal grandfather John Boyle started working in the Homestead plant as a water boy in 1918. When he went to collect his pay, the boss denied hiring him, and said to come back next week if he wanted a job. "That must have been an initiation rite for kids because the same thing happened to my mother's father," says Bonnie, "only his mother was depending on his money and beat the tar out of him."

Only recently, Bonnie discovered that John Boyle's mother Ida Mae Carroll, who died at his birth, was a second cousin of Charles Carroll, the only Roman Catholic and the richest man to sign the *Declaration of Independence*. Such lineage would have been beyond the imagination of John Boyle, whose only way out of poverty was to enter a steel mill in the worst of times.

While Big Steel appeared to be the victor when the strike ended on January 8, 1920, the solidarity of workers increased. The repression of their civil rights and the efforts to keep them divided by ethnicity inspired unity. The hunkies, among others, saw glimmers of new possibilities, even though new advances would not be made until the Depression.

"For a long time after the Hunky Strike, you still couldn't mention the word *union*," Steve Brozek said. As a teenager with high hopes, he joined the labor gang and trudged with his father to the Edgar Thomson Works, their lunches wrapped in newspapers. They worked sixty- to seventy-hour weeks, sometimes starting and finishing in the dark. "After a while I say to myself, 'hey this gotta go.' And I began putting two and two together because I was working with different gangs. Had an Italian gang . . . and a black gang. An Irish gang. So when I worked with these old-timers, I thought, my God . . . they're puttin' all their life in here. This thing has to be changed. And I always looked forward to that."

Chapter 3

✺☙✺

Spies, Prejudice and Poverty
If you wasn't Irish, you didn't get a job.

During the Great Depression, men who held middle-management, white-collar jobs inside the mills were either threatened or lionized for the power they had. Eugene Shatlock, whose ties to Homestead predate 1892, showed me a gun that had been rigged to shoot anyone who came out the back door of his family's home. Pulling the highly polished gun from a wool sweat sock, Eugene set it carefully on a lace tablecloth while his wife, Isabel, and I watched. Eugene's father, Paul, a personnel officer in the industrial relations department of the Homestead Works, had been responsible for assigning work hours. "Dad would fill the positions needed for the next day, maybe a machinist's helper or someone at the open hearth. He was seen as the guy who would determine who would make enough money to get along to the next payday." A disgruntled steelworker fixed a gun on the porch so that it would harm any Shatlock who opened the door. "That just shows what the attitude was," Eugene shakes his head. "The guy just went over the edge, but thankfully the gun didn't go off."

Desperate wives brought homemade baked goods to the Shatlocks' home, begging Paul to assign work to their husbands. "But he wouldn't take anything," Eugene insists. After her father-in-law died, Isabel recalls, an older woman said that her family had considered Paul a "saint" because he kept their father working during the Depression.

Mary Howat, 88, a retired librarian, whose father was payroll clerk, says he always wore a tie, but if a worker admired it, he was quick to say "want it?" and give it away, a *noblesse oblige* gesture often creating more tension than it relieved.

The hard days of the Depression are still sharp memories for steelworkers who lived through them. Sitting on their screened porch overlooking their summer garden, John and Evelyn Hrika, with their dear friend Alex Savko, remember when flowers and fresh vegetables were absent from their lives. John's father came to Homestead from Slovakia in 1923 in search of a better life. Seven years later, he had enough money for his wife and three children to join him. "Unfortunately, we came here at the beginning of the Depression, and my father worked in the open hearth. Sometimes he wouldn't work for a couple months, only maybe a day or two—so we lived for a while in two rooms, close to the mill." John watched his father and friends draw straws to see who would win a workday.

"If you didn't work very much, one day a month or so, the company had a center where you could pick up a box of food, different kinds of basic foods like potatoes and cheese," Alex adds. "We used to go with our wagon and pick it up. But you'd be surprised. Whenever you got paid and went back to work, the company kept records, and you had to pay for those things."

Hunger and poverty were so rampant that steelworkers became more "bold" about meeting publicly, Steve Brozek describes in an oral interview for the Rivers of Steel National Heritage Area. Having accomplished very little through secret meetings in private homes or ethnic clubs, union advocates became more visible in their efforts. Brozek and Joe Payne, with support from the Amalgamated Association of Iron, Steel and Tin Workers, rented a storeroom in the heart of Braddock and helped to organize Local 1219 of the United Steel Workers of America. Brozek spoke Polish, Slovak and Croation, which helped him gain the support of old-time Slavs and Poles willing to pay monthly dues of 25 cents and risk their jobs. The steel company didn't break up the meetings, but foremen watched from parked cars and wrote down names, Brozek said. But five years after U. S. Steel recognized the union, in 1937, Payne still recruited members to the USWA surreptitiously by arriving at the mill before his shift to distribute applications. To avoid calling too much attention to himself, he signed them when he got home.

Steve Brozek recalled his days as a union organizer in a letter he wrote to Anna Marie Sninsky, dated January 25, 1993. After reading that she was president of the Associated Artists of Pittsburgh, he recognized her as the daughter of Bill Jacko, a major dynamo in the drive to organize steelworkers in the early '30s. Jacko was president of Local 1219 in 1940, and Brozek was recording secretary. When Jacko, a talented musician, was 19, he had given Brozek, then 12, violin lessons.

"Our immigrant parents," Brozek wrote to Sninsky, "believe that their children should have a better life, so one day my dad came home with a violin [thinking] I should be a musician and that [our] neighbor Bill Jacko should teach me."

William A. C. Jacko's father, Andrew, had emigrated to Braddock from Austria-Hungary to get a job at Edgar Thomson. From the day Bill was born, Andrew and his wife Julia had high aspirations for him. In 1927 he graduated summa cum laude from Carnegie Institute of Technology (now Carnegie Mellon University) with a degree in chemical engineering. Bill worked his way through college while at Edgar Thomson, where he grew up only doors away from the main entrance. Yet when he began an engineering career in the laboratory of ET, he was consistently passed over for managerial promotions because of his "ethnic heritage," says Anna Marie, which spurred him to become a union organizer, concentrating on workers' rights. Philip Murray, president of the United Steel Workers of America, requested a leave of absence for him from ET in 1943 and appointed him to the International Staff of the USWA, where he later became the director of the Wage Division, often interceding in international disputes.

A banner headline on the front page of the Homestead *Daily Messenger* reported Jacko's death on June 17, 1965.

Different from Bill Jacko, Joe Payne was not from an Eastern European family, but he too was drawn to the union because of prejudice that hurt him and his wallet. He earned $20 a week as a new steelworker at ET in 1936. But he didn't understand why every payday "a guy down the mill" asked to borrow $15 from him. Joe's mother finally revealed that Italian friends who owned a bar had bought Joe his job for $15 and as part of the deal, had promised the boss $15 every payday. "When I heard that, I says, 'I'm gonna go out for the union.' And I did. I never gave that guy nothin'."

But the boss continued to collect a case of beer every week from Joe's sponsors. "I seen him one day in there [the bar]. And I'm representative of the union. And I got hold of Nick and I said, 'you don't have to give that guy a case of beer anymore. This is the United States.'"

Joe and the boss "got into it at the mill. I said, 'listen you big hunky you. I'll stick a needle in your belly and let the air out!' He tried to get me fired, but I was a little too smart for him. But that $15 bothered me . . . [The hunky] who asked for the $15 said, 'I'm gonna climb and you guys are gonna put me there.' And he did, but he was no good. If you'd only know how many of them Dagos paid off for their jobs. Including my old man. . . ."

Despite this experience, Joe still thought he could follow his dream and become a carpenter at ET. He called the carpentry shop about an ad and was encouraged to stop by and fill out an application. When he arrived, the guy said, "we're not taking any applications now—all filled up."

A month later, another carpenter told him what really had happened. On the telephone *Payne* sounded Anglo-Saxon, "but that face of yours is the map of Italy. You know what you were, a white nigger." And Payne knows his informant was right. Italians never worked in the carpentry shop and were sent to the track gang with Blacks and Mexicans. Payne is proud that "the union stopped all that. We're the ones who stopped it. I was part of that and so was Stanley, and Bill Jacko."

But unionizing was not a cure-all for ethnic bias. John Hrika recalls a "Johnny Bull," an English foreman, saying, "'I'm going to fire those two guys because I don't like Dagos.' They were father and son—good workers, loaded ladles—but he fired them," Hrika told me.

Sons and daughters of Italian steelworkers still ache when recalling the verbal abuse suffered by their fathers. "My dad was a perfectionist, a cement worker," Gerry Boccella describes her father, Michael Rosella. "He was well read in science and literature, knew opera and often translated Dante for professors at the university. He'd come home from the mill and tell my mother how he was much better educated than any of the guys who were over him, but he had a family to support and was careful about showing any anger."

"Down at ET when you started there or you was a kid, your nationality made all the difference," admits Jim Boland, a proud Irishman, who relished his job in the open hearth. "That and the rolling mills were the biggest paying jobs. The rest of them departments, there wasn't any money, unless for machinists."

Starting as a kid at eighteen in 1939, earning 80 cents an hour, Boland worked his way up from the labor gang to a general foreman. [During the Depression], "if you wasn't Irish, you didn't get a job, and you better be Catholic. All the big-shot maintenance guys were Catholic. Bricklayers were all Scotch. The Italians worked in the track gang, the lowest job, and the Slavs was in maintenance. . . . No one discriminated against religion like U. S. Steel did. Because you only went so far. You'd go to assistant general superintendent. And if a superintendent's job opened, no Catholic got it. You had to be a Shriner. In the '40s, the unions got tired of that . . . and it all changed."

The union had also a role in an earlier change, which led to an improved wage scale with fewer hours. By passing the Wagner Act in 1935, a Democratic Congress responsive to unions granted them the right to organize and gave workers the right to bargain collectively. This New Deal legislation, the depressed economy, and the receptivity of the workers resulted in a visit to the Steel Valley in 1936 from Philip Murray, the leader of the Steel Workers Organizing Committee (SWOC), seeking members to organize by industry instead of craft. Although Steel Valley people favored unions, they distrusted outsiders because of the failures of 1892 and 1919. But the SWOC leadership gained support and trust through persistence, innovation and appeals in the native languages of the Slovaks, Hungarians, Polish and Italians. On March 2, 1937, their tactics paid off. U. S. Steel upset a tradition of more than forty years since the Homestead Strike by recognizing an outside union. It granted a five-day week and eight-hour day. It granted wage increases for common labor and promised increases for skilled and semi-skilled workers, plus a time and a half rate for overtime.

For steelworker Bill O'Leary, father of five children, whose story the *New York World-Telegram* followed, this meant annual pay of $2,500, an increase of $1,000 over what he had earned the year before.

As unions gained more influence and a Democratic Congress supported labor, steelworkers' lives continued to improve. But even though job descriptions and a seniority system became more standardized, ethnic divisiveness was apparent as late as the '50s. One steelworker recalls seeing an Italian bricklayer and his son, "good workers," called "guinea and wop" to their faces by an Irish foreman. And life in the mill continued to be a struggle for African-Americans, although they had a long history in the steel industry. Genuine progress for black workers lagged decades behind advances for white workers.

African-American workers were imported from the South during the Strike of 1919 to keep the mills going. That year, 14,610 black steelworkers were in Pittsburgh, according to Dennis C. Dickerson in *Out of the Crucible: Black Steelworkers in Western Pennsylvania, 1875-1980.*

One of them was Annie Morgan's husband who worked in a tobacco factory in Richmond for a dollar a day in 1917. "[The mill] brought him up here—my husband and some of his friends—and put them in what they called 'the bunkhouse,' a place . . . near the [Edgar Thomson] mill . . . and they stayed down there until they could find someplace for their families," Annie Morgan, 80, told David Demarest in an interview for the Braddock Field's Historical Society in 1999.

"He was working there when the union came to organize—I think [it] was 1919. They would go in the mill and stay there sometimes two or three days. [The mill] told the men they brought in that if they continued working, they would pay them double wages. After the strike was over, of course, they joined the union, and he belonged to the union until he died. . . ."

Annie's husband worked in the blast furnace "for a long time" until he couldn't stand the heat. When he died in 1944, he was still a laborer in the mill.

Until the '70s, most Blacks had hot and dirty jobs. To be second helper on a furnace was the best they could hope for. "We didn't have any jobs like bricklayers. No skilled jobs. Blacks might be hired, but we weren't promoted. We were stuck in what were called 'Black jobs'—cleaning out sewers and punching checkers," says Ramón Reid, 72, who once worked at Edgar Thomson.

As a "checker" he had to go underneath the furnace, and climb into and clean out hundreds of holes, twenty-feet deep that were clogged with soot, dirt and slag. The heat was intense and the job endless. After working only a year, he left ET at the time of the civil rights movement, disappointing his father who had spent his life there and who still believes Ramón would have become a boss if he had stayed because "things were beginning to change."

John Mitchell Reid, Ramón's father, loved the mill. Sitting across from me at the Carnegie Library of Swissvale, Ramón—soft-spoken for a former amateur middleweight boxer—lights up talking about his dad, who's now ninety-four. "When I was a kid, I thought he must have had fun down there because he was always rarin' to go," Ramón laughs. "Segregation was bad in the mill, but he had a good personality and got along with both black and white."

John Reid left a "hot job" because he couldn't stand the heat, and spent years in the stockyard checking trucks and trains going in and out. The job suited him because he was a high school graduate, so his reading, writing and math skills were superior to most steelworkers' at that time, even those who made better money. To support his family, John Reid always had two jobs. After getting home from a shift, he'd go off to paint houses or repair roofs.

Similar to John Reid, Judge Cynthia Baldwin's father, James Alexander Ackron, had completed eleventh grade when starting at National Tube, in McKeesport, in 1929. In her chambers at the City-County Building in Pittsburgh, she told me about a supervisor saying to him, "If it were up to me, I'd promote you to foreman, but no way can I make you a boss over white people. They won't stand for it." Instead, a man with a sixth-grade education got the job. But the sympathetic supervisor made Ackron a diesel engineer, where he could work independently, and be responsible for hauling materials by rail throughout the mill.

Judge Baldwin describes her father as a "pragmatist. He knew he had to work, so he'd take stands but not make trouble." In forty-six years, he missed only six days at the mill. "The mill made a wonderful life for us, mostly because my father was a hard worker. He'd call home and say, 'I'm going to stay on for the next shift, so don't worry about me.'" He had even arranged his wedding to take place between shifts.

As a child, Judge Baldwin was impressed that her father read three daily newspapers and devoured Zane Grey novels. "There was never an option that I wouldn't go to college," she says. And her father lived to see her become a judge before he died at ninety-two. Since we talked, Judge Baldwin was appointed to the Supreme Court of Pennsylvania.

Like many others in the Steel Valley, Judge Baldwin grew up in an integrated street where Irish, Slovaks, Hungarians and African-Americans were in an out of each other's homes. Kids walked to school together and mothers dropped off homemade soups and stews when someone was sick. Ethnic and religious diversity was generally respected in neighborhoods, even when such tolerance was not transferred to the mills or the bars by their husbands and fathers. For example, after finishing a shift, African-Americans were not welcome to drink in white men's bars. If a black man were served, the bartender would break his glass or wash it with salt and water.

Some steelworkers think that the union from the very beginning should have taken a stronger position on racial and ethnic discrimination. Ray Henderson, an African-American, insists he didn't let many things bother him at Edgar Thomson after World War II because Slavs and Italians were also shut out from jobs. "You're no better off than I am, no different except that your skin is white," he'd tell them. "You're fighting the same problems I'm fighting."

"The unions did lots of good," Henderson says in an oral history he gave in 1992 for the Rivers of Steel National Heritage Area, but he also notes that they allowed the rollers and the first helpers to be exclusively white, barred Blacks from union leadership and let workers be segregated into groups. Because black workers were hired after the Korean War and again in the late '60s, they gained seniority by the late '70s. But white workers and bosses still met in ethnic clubs and bars to plot against them, according to Henderson. "Talk to them now, and they admit it, but not at the time. The bosses had access to the seniority lists and could strategize using them."

Jim Boland gave me an example of how foremen had ways of maneuvering Blacks to suit their prejudices. Four African-Americans worked in the open hearth of the ET plant when he left for the Navy in World War II. When he returned in 1945, the plant "was loaded with them because there was nobody else around." But Boland said he never had to work with Blacks because "the turn I come from, our fellas kept them off. . . . [Our foreman] wouldn't keep none on his turn. . . . They were all on [another foreman's] turn. And then they just moved up seniority like anybody else," a contention Henderson would challenge.

The reality is that most Blacks were locked into a laborer's salary, making it hard to buy a car or take a family vacation. "People who went back down home, that worked in the mills for years, had to save a whole year just to get gas money to go home and come back in an old raggedy car," says Henderson. "The union could have stopped all that—if they wanted to—but didn't until the end," when they wanted to present a united front to the steel companies.

Although wages were low for black men in the mill, "they were the best they could get and the jobs were prized, even if they weren't that great. I don't think there was ever a black roller," says Evelyn Benzo, 78, the widow of a former millworker and the daughter-in-law of Wilbur Benzo, the first African-American superintendent, and the head of maintenance workers, at Edgar Thomson prior to the civil rights movement. Evelyn's husband, Ramón Benzo, worked for ten years as a bricklayer's helper until he had a heart attack in the early '60s and became a salesman for Sears.

Evelyn and I talked in a meeting room at the Carnegie Library in Braddock, built for steelworkers and their families and dedicated in 1889, the first of 1,679 libraries built by Andrew Carnegie in the United States. Now in the process of extensive renovation after years of neglect, the Library originally provided the community with athletic and shower facilities, an exquisite auditorium, and a swimming pool in addition to books. As a child, Evelyn loved finding a quiet corner in the Library and reading. "I could enjoy it all, except the swimming pool. Blacks weren't allowed. To this day I can't swim. But I've always said the Library saved Carnegie's soul."

Serving her third term in Braddock Council, Benzo thinks that if "young people had to go through some of these things, they might be more appreciative now." She doesn't dwell on the past, but says, "millwork required discipline. For the most part, Blacks had the hottest, dirtiest jobs, but if you wanted to work, you worked, even if you didn't like what you did. It was a sign of the times. It was hard for black men to get jobs they qualified for or have any hope for doing much better."

Richard Ford, 56, followed his two grandfathers into the mill in 1967, and became the first African-American journeyman electronic repairman at the Clairton Works. He never saw his chances for promotion as being different from anyone else's until he scored low on an objective test and a disappointed superintendent said "he had a large herd riding on me. I guess there was opposition to me, but I didn't know it until then."

As we talked in South Side Hospital where he was recovering from knee surgery, not far from where the Jones & Laughlin plant once stood, Ford explained why he left the steel industry after seven years and went with the International Brotherhood of Electrical Workers, despite his father's opposition. "Not just because of the pay—I went from $5.20 an hour in the mill to $10 with the union—but I just couldn't imagine working in the mill year after year with the same people. It was just so narrow to me. I wanted to see and do more, and the Brotherhood gave me a chance to work in different places, different states."

By the time the Homestead plant shut down in 1986, Blacks "were pretty integrated," says Mike Stout, a grievance officer for the union. "I mean they had to fight and struggle over a number of years and file lawsuits, but, I mean, we were a family. Going into the mill was like having a whole other family."

If so, this was not the experience of Robert Gibb. In a quiet tone that tempers his anger, he describes the mill as "incredibly hateful and racist . . . yet the kindest people were invariably the Blacks who were being dumped on by everybody else. They were all the way down and spent all their lives as janitors."

In general, steelworkers had an inbred suspicion of education because many didn't finish high school. "They'd rather dig a ditch than write anything down on a piece of paper," says Martin Conners, a veteran of many Steel Valley plants. "They were satisfied to have the job they had. Many of them weren't too capable of moving up."

In this environment, an African-American steelworker was an important influence on Gibb. Often the target of personal hostility for reading books on his lunch break, he would find them "ripped apart, strewn about, stuck with grease." But one day while Gibb was reading and eating "this older black man who didn't know me from Adam, came over and said to me—a white guy—'what are you doing here? You got to go to college. You gotta get outta here if you don't want to spend your lifetime.' And God knows how he was treated every day, but he's telling me I should have something better than him, and I'm looking around at all these other people who seemed to want him to have nothing. Not anything near to what they could have."

Genuine advances for African-Americans are more recent and evident in the career of Alvina King, 42, now a "pusher" and "gang leader" in the Clairton Works. Starting in the mill in 1997, she moved up through the ranks by learning to work all of the equipment necessary for holding these positions. But first she had to be able to tolerate extreme degrees of heat, which not all steelworkers are able to do. A pusher shoves coal into a hot oven and pushes it out when it reduces to coke, a necessary ingredient for producing steel. As gang leader, Alvina gives workers their breaks and then operates their machines so that production doesn't miss a beat.

To qualify as a gang leader—"not many people know how to run all of the machines," Alvina explains. At first, the machines were intimidating to her, but "running them is so awesome. That's the challenge and the satisfaction," she says. Besides that, she runs the pushing machine from an air-conditioned cab that protects her from rain, cold and heat. "You're more in fire and smoke in other jobs, so that's another good part about moving up. But the more you move up on the machines, the better the pay—so that's another incentive," she adds.

Male steelworkers admire her skills and helped her learn the machines. She's the only woman in the crew of eighteen men. "But no one's ignorant or nasty about my being a woman," she says, although she does sit on the Civil Rights Committee dealing with harassment issues.

For Black History Month, March 2000, the plant newsletter called attention to a historical occasion because two women—African-Americans—were operating pusher machinery at the same time. Alvina King and Sheri Robison were given plaques for working "efficiently, effectively and expertly"—praise and opportunities their forbearers were seldom granted.

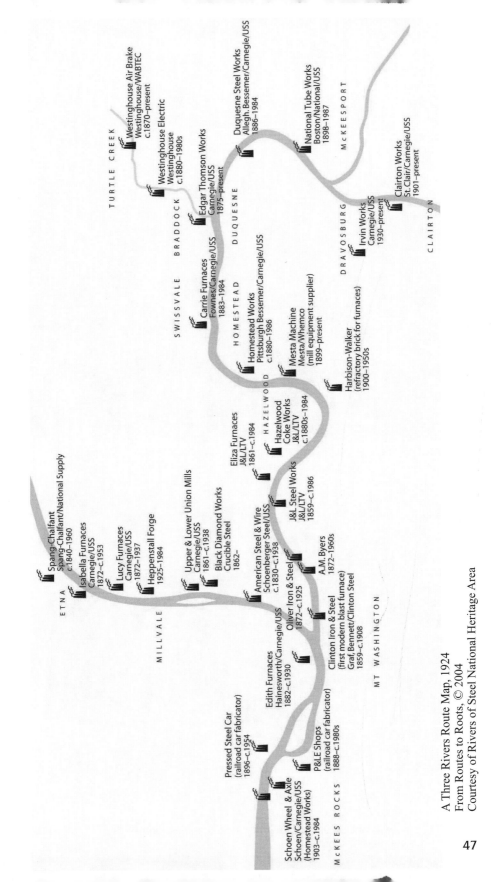

TURTLE CREEK

Westinghouse Air Brake
Westinghouse/WABTEC
c.1870–present

Westinghouse Electric
Westinghouse
c.1880–1980s

BRADDOCK

Edgar Thomson Works
Carnegie/USS
1875–present

Duquesne Steel Works
Allegh. Bessemer/Carnegie/USS
1886–1984

National Tube Works
Boston/National/USS
1898–1987

McKEESPORT

Carrie Furnaces
Fownes/Carnegie/USS
1883–1984

Clairton Works
St. Clair/Carnegie/USS
1901–present

SWISSVALE

DUQUESNE

CLAIRTON

HOMESTEAD

Homestead Works
Pittsburgh Bessemer/Carnegie/USS
c.1880–1986

DRAVOSBURG

Irvin Works
Carnegie/USS
1930–present

Mesta Machine
Mesta/Whemco
(mill equipment supplier)
1899–present

Harbison-Walker
(refractory brick for furnaces)
1900–1950s

Eliza Furnaces
J&L/LTV
1861–c.1984

HAZELWOOD

Hazelwood
Coke Works
J&L/LTV
c.1880s–1984

Spang-Chalfant
Spang-Chalfant/National Supply
c.1840–1960

Isabella Furnaces
Carnegie/USS
1872–c.1953

Lucy Furnaces
Carnegie/USS
1872–1937

Heppenstall Forge
1925–1984

Upper & Lower Union Mills
Carnegie/USS
1861–c.1938

Black Diamond Works
Crucible Steel
1862–

J&L Steel Works
J&L/LTV
1859–c.1986

ETNA

MILLVALE

American Steel & Wire
Schoenberger Steel/USS
c.1830–1938

Oliver Iron & Steel
1872–c.1925

A.M. Byers
1872–1960s

Clinton Iron & Steel
(first modern blast furnace)
Graf, Bennett/Clinton Steel
1859–c.1908

MT WASHINGTON

Edith Furnaces
Hainesworth/Carnegie/USS
1882–c.1930

Pressed Steel Car
(railroad car fabricator)
1896–c.1954

P&LE Shops
(railroad car fabricator)
1888–c.1980s

Schoen Wheel & Axle
Schoen/Carnegie/USS
(Homestead Works)
1903–c.1984

McKEES ROCKS

A Three Rivers Route Map, 1924
From Routes to Roots, © 2004
Courtesy of Rivers of Steel National Heritage Area

LUKE SWANK [Filling Molds with Molten Iron] c. 1934
Photo courtesy of Carnegie Library of Pittsburgh

LUKE SWANK [End of shift, 4 p.m., 1942]
Courtesy of William J. Gaughan Collection, Archives Service Center,
University of Pittsburgh

HARPER'S WEEKLY
A JOURNAL OF CIVILIZATION

Vol. XXXVI.—No. 1856.
Copyright, 1892, by Harper & Brothers.
All Rights Reserved.

NEW YORK, SATURDAY, JULY 16, 1892.

TEN CENTS A COPY.
FOUR DOLLARS A YEAR.

Harper's Weekly cover, 1892
Courtesy of Rivers of Steel National Heritage Area

49

LUKE SWANK [Interior of Cast House, Molten Pig Iron and Runners] c. 1930; vintage gelatin silver print 10 x 13 5/16 in. Courtesy of Carnegie Museum of Art, Pittsburgh: Gift of Edith Swank Long by transfer from the Pennsylvania Department, Carnegie Library of Pittsburgh

[Hillside Houses Stand on One Another's Shoulders, as if jostling for a view of Jones & Laughlin Steel Mill off of Second Ave. c. 1940s]
Courtesy of Carnegie Library of Pittsburgh

[Open Hearth furnace crew early 1900s, Pittsburgh Works]
Courtesy of Library and Archives Division, Historical Society
of Western Pennsylvania, Pittsburgh, PA

51

LUKE SWANK [Two Women, Laundry and Graffiti] c. 1938; vintage silver print
7 9/16 x 9 3/8 in.
Courtesy of Carnegie Museum of Art, Pittsburgh: Gift of Edith Swank Long by transfer
from the Pennsylvania Department, Carnegie Library of Pittsburgh

[Woman Welding Beams, January 24, 1945, Carnegie-Illinois Steel
Corporation. Homestead Steel Works]
Courtesy of William J. Gaughan Collection, Archives Service Center,
University of Pittsburgh

[Female Employees at Carrie Furnace, October 1944, Bethlehem Steel
Corporation. Rankin Works. Carrie Furnace]
Courtesy of William J. Gaughan Collection, Archives Service Center,
University of Pittsburgh

LUKE SWANK [Three Boys in a Wagon] c. 1934; vintage silver print 10 5/16 x 13 1/16 in.
Courtesy of Carnegie Museum of Art, Pittsburgh: Gift of Edith Swank Long by transfer
from the Pennsylvania Department, Carnegie Library of Pittsburgh

Part 2:
The Mills' Grip on Women and Children

Chapter 4

Building a Life Around Shifts

You were on call 24 hours a day.

Steelworkers' wives pummeled Pinkerton guards during the Homestead Strike of 1892 and shouted at mounted Iron and Steel Police on Braddock streets during the Hunky Strike of 1919. During the Great Depression, they walked across bridges and up steep hills to clean houses in affluent neighborhoods, only to repeat the same tasks in their own homes at night. Some women replaced their husbands in steel plants during World War II, but returned to their kitchens when it ended. Always skeptical about the future, they hid "strike money" in coffee cans and flour tins. And better than their husbands working in the mills, they lived in harmony in ethnic neighborhoods.

Whatever the decade, the mill occupied the center of their lives, sometimes provoking their revolutionary spirit and political voice. But the larger reality is that the mill defined women in relation to the physical, psychological and emotional needs of husbands who worked for a controlling and powerful industry.

The ultimate challenge for a mill wife's understanding was dramatized daily when 5,000 workers spilled out of the Homestead plant at 8 A.M., 4 P.M. and midnight. In earlier times, when steelworkers were paid in cash, their wives, wearing babushkas, waited at the "hole in the wall," the paymasters tunnel, to claim the lion's share of their husband's meager salaries. Years later, wives in pink hair rollers and chenille robes drove up to the mill, demanding that husbands fork over their checks before cashing and squandering them in neighborhood bars.

"It was macho. You were expected to go to the bar, no matter the shift," says Martin Conners. But after working at the Clairton Works, he understood why steelworkers gulped down boilermakers. "Spicy foods like strong coffee, kielbasa or whiskey are all you can taste because the dirt and gas from the oven cause you to lose your sense of taste and smell. But guys also drank whiskey going into work at 7 in the morning, just to make it through the day. We didn't realize it then, but it was alcoholism. A learned habit."

"If you saw a shift change, even once, you'd never forget it," says Ray Bodnar, a former steelworker and now mayor of West Mifflin, an area that wraps around Homestead. "The men were grimy and sweaty and had to have that shot and beer. They deserved it, especially on a hot day."

Saloons and the steel mills prospered together. As early as 1917, Mrs. Samuel Hamilton, a Braddock resident, observed "When the great steel mill [Edgar Thomson] was planted at the head of Thirteenth Street, Braddock, it brought with its prosperity man's curse, woman's enemy and the children's education in vice and crime—the saloon."

Night and day, saloons in river towns accommodated the changing of shifts. Drinks were set up ahead of time, ready for the rush. "You knew what each one drank. But mostly they wanted boilermakers, a shot of whiskey washed down with a small glass of beer," says Lorraine Novak, owner of Novak's Tavern, a popular watering hole in Duquesne for steelworkers and mill bosses. Even early in the morning, boilermakers were the drink of choice. "Men said the whiskey cleared their lungs and the beer softened the whiskey. Well, if they did, I don't know," shrugs Lorraine, folding her arms across an embroidered sweatshirt as people with coffee mugs pass by us in the all-purpose room of the Duquesne Borough Building, where she is Town Controller.

"I never ran into any trouble with guys coming into the bar. Most of them were regulars, but I'd lose patience listening to the same stories," Lorraine offers. "I loved when the World Series was on because everybody would shut their mouth and watch."

But Steel Valley bars were seldom quiet. Straka's Tavern, known for robust home-cooked food and stacked roast beef sandwiches, closed only between 2 and 6 A.M. "Once you made a customer, you kept him," says Millie Tarasevich, 79, Joe Straka's daughter. Joe opened the tavern with his mother-in-law during the Depression and watched it flourish after Prohibition in 1932. He arrived at 6 A.M. to slice all the meats, and the short-order cook and two bartenders came in soon after that. "By 7:10 we'd have a bar full of steelworkers drinking and eating, but they didn't consider it breakfast because they had worked all night," Millie tells me while pouring herbal tea into fragile tea cups at her dining room table.

Steelworkers' wives preferred Straka's to other bars because their husbands were likely to eat stuffed cabbage, meatloaf or haluski and not just guzzle boilermakers, and because Joe Straka would send men home or call their wives if they were drunk. On paydays, Straka's kept thousands of dollars available for cashing checks at every shift. When wives trailed their husbands there, they left the men an allowance for the night, and headed home.

Even children showed up sometimes to capture some of the paycheck before it all went for drinks. For example, as a little girl, the youngest of nine children, Martha Sloan checked out the bars on paydays, looking for her father. *Dai mi panejik* ("Give me your money") her mother taught her to say in Slovak. Then Martha wrapped the cash tightly in a handkerchief and ran two miles home.

Now 69, Martha remembers that she "did this week after week because that's what we had to live on. Otherwise, the money was spent at the bar and we couldn't pay the 'tick' at the grocer's. We had soup three times a week, so every day we'd buy a pound of soup bones or whatever, and we just kept adding to the tick. Come payday, we were expected to pay on it."

After a night at the bar, Martha's father would sit in their backyard by the water pump, begging his wife's forgiveness, by singing, "*dushichka Annichkastonicka*" ("my heart, Annie") to sweet Slovak melodies. "Oh, I can hear him now," Martha sighs. "The more he sang, the madder she got."

One of Martha's favorite stories about growing up with mill kids is about a friend's father who never remembered what happened after he drank heavily. Fed up with his stumbling through the door after the 4 to midnight shift, his wife hit him in the face with an iron skillet, breaking his nose. "'Man, I must have been in a helluva fight,'" he said the next morning.'" But his wife told him that he had fallen down the concrete steps into the house, and that she had nursed him.

Women settled their scores in devious ways because they couldn't risk the life they had for an unknown future. And men, dominated by work schedules and repetitive labor, seized chances for any escape. The result was often irresolvable but muted conflict.

For example, an eighty-year-old widow, a former Rosie the Riveter, had little sympathy when her husband arrived home drunk in the wee hours of the morning, long after his shift ended. "I was frying bacon and eggs for him and just threw the whole skillet against the wall. Eggs and bacon grease were splattered all over the kitchen. The next morning he was so apologetic. Thought we had some kind of cooking accident, and I let him believe that for years, she confesses with glee as we chat at BRAVO!, a restaurant that occupies part of the site where the production floor of the Homestead Works used to be, and where she worked sixty years ago as a messenger.

While most wives preferred their husbands working the daylight shift, and some men found the midnight to 8 "graveyard" shift slow and boring, others like Roy Gottschalk, a twenty-year mill veteran when the Homestead plant closed in 1986, liked working 4 to midnight because it was easier to "squeeze in an extra hour at the bar before heading home." Mill kids often liked this shift because their mothers were "off duty" for the evening, Janis Dofner, Director of Communications at the Rivers of Steel National Heritage Area, told me. "My mother didn't have to have dinner on the table. She'd say 'let's go shopping' and we'd just open a can of soup and take off."

Midnight was the worst shift, Anne Pcholinsky says. For thirty-eight years, she planned around her husband Johnny's shifts at Jones & Laughlin where he had a hot and dangerous job as a scarfer. He burned impurities from steel with torches, and often ignited himself in the process.

Johnny had to ride two trolleys for an hour and a half to get to work. "On the midnight shift that was really tough in the winter," Anne allows. "But after his shift, he'd stop at a bar. Then he'd get off the trolley and stop at our neighborhood bar. So it was a long time before he settled down, ate, argued and then went to bed and slept all afternoon. I'd have to keep the children very quiet until he got up and it was time to leave again."

"I don't deny that his job was hazardous and demanding," says Anne, "but he always had that bottle of moonshine on the table. Had to get rid of the impurities and have a drink. 'I deserve it.' That's what they always said. I guess the only way men had to relax was to go out drinking with their buddies."

If her children were to have a better life, Anne knew she had to take positive action. She joined a therapy group to learn more about alcoholism and focused on the children's future. "If they got an education I felt they'd see they didn't have to follow in their father's footsteps." And she was successful in accomplishing that.

"Steelworkers had a tough life," Anne insists. "They'd be soaking wet in the summer, but women worked just as hard, and aren't given much credit."

Steelworkers' wives were always fenced-in by the schedule of the mills. "You were on call twenty-four hours a day," says Pat Seybert, the daughter and wife of steelworkers. "You never got any rest. Kids came home from school and you'd get them all night by yourself. Then your husband comes home at midnight and is rarin' to go, and so you're not asleep until 2 A.M. Then you're up with the kids at 6 or 7. You were more tired than he was."

Wives prepared meals at various hours because shifts sometimes changed every three days. A man needing to be at the mill by 4 would eat a big dinner at 2 or 3 in the afternoon. School children coming home at 4 generally ate at 5. Husbands getting home at midnight sat down to another home-cooked meal, or at least warmed leftovers.

"Everybody's life was turned around on 4 to midnight. I hated 4 to midnight," Pat throws up her hands even at the thought of it. "I still can't imagine people eating dinner at 8 o'clock. I think people in this area still eat at 4 or 5:30 at the latest. We're still tied into the mill schedule."

Wives did experience shifts differently from their husbands, but don't always say so. When I spoke with the Bolands, a retired mill couple, and asked Jim what he missed most about working, Rose answered for him: "*After the mill*," he liked best. He looked forward to the time *after*."

Jim, unabashed, agrees. "Especially night turn. Like you'd come out of work at 7:30 A.M. and then maybe drink until one o'clock; go home, get up for supper at 5; maybe take another couple hours of sleep, and then leave for work around 10 o'clock. Some mills had shifts at 7 A.M., 3 and 11 P.M."

Jim never ate breakfast when coming off a shift at 7 A.M. He drank and kibitzed at the bar until Rose picked him up. "Then we'd go for lunch or breakfast or whatever you call it, before I'd take him home," Rose nods. One time after work, she remembers him saying, "'I wish I was just goin' to start my turn.' He just liked it that much." Jim agrees that the camaraderie was tops.

He kept a calendar, crossing off the days he had to work daylight. "He wanted day turns out of the way for the month," Rose explains. But when I ask what shifts were like for *her* when their family was young, Rose looks startled.

"Me!? Well, when he was daylight, 7 to 3, he'd get the kids up for school and I used to sleep most of the day because I'd stay up all night washing the kids' clothes." Rose seems to be more comfortable talking about Jim's schedule than her own, perhaps because her preferences are opposite to his. The daylight shift gave Rose a chance to "get out to bingos in the evening because he was home. Bingos and talking to friends were my entertainment." But when Jim worked 3 to 11 and got home well after midnight, "I'd be cooking," Rose says. "I always cooked a meal when he came in." And finally, "But I never complained. I never envied anybody for what they have."

From 1945 until July 31, 1961, the day of her husband's funeral, Ruth Haas, a mill wife, kept track of her husband's shifts at the Irvin Works in little lined notebooks, the kind banks and insurance agencies once gave as practical Christmas gifts. Now 89, Ruth looks at the diaries for 1958, 1959 and 1961 stacked on her daughter's kitchen table, and can't remember confiding in any of them. Yet her written words, stripped of emotion and reflection, capture the routine schedule of a steelworker's family. Her sparse style accepts the way things are. She controls her days by noting the weather, the hours her husband Ted works, the food she prepares and the clothes she washes, starches and irons for seven children. She calls it a "good day" when all the children are in school and she finished her housework, only to begin again the next morning.

Pleasures are small ones. She savors a ride to the Dairy Queen with Ted; likes buying three housedresses on a Saturday afternoon, and is delighted to win $4.00 at bingo. Family conflicts are seldom mentioned, except those that promise quick healing.

> *Saturday, February 1, 1958* Cleaned today. Kids o.k. but Ted went to hit John for picking his nose & his ear. John complaining about his ear. Thelma and Jim went sled riding. He ran over her finger with the sled. Everything o.k. Watching t.v. Went to Thorofare for 2 frying chickens.

A typical format is

> *Monday, January 13, 1958* Kids all in school, except John and Sandy. Ted works 4-12 [. . . .] washed clothes after Ted went to work [. . . .] kids all in bed by 10:30. Ted shellacked the toy cupboard doors today.

When the ironing isn't finished, Ruth promises herself to catch up.

> *Wednesday, April 2* Ted works 8-4. All kids in school today. Ironed all day today starched some [. . . .] didn't finish but will do it tomorrow.

Thanksgiving dinner is planned around Ted's shift.

> *Thursday, November 26, 1959* Roast turkey apple pie (1) pumpkin pie (5) mashed potatoes, candied sweet potatoes, macaroni salad, jello with fruit (salad – lettuce, tomatoes, cucumbers) stuffing, gravy, 2 kinds of cranberries, coffee, coke, olives, pickles, celery, radishes. Cooked turkey all nite on 200 until 5 came down & shut it off went back to bed till 9. Finished all at 11 and got everyone up for turkey dinner. Ted 4-12.

Ruth's daughter, Sandy Doby, 48, also a mill wife, leafing through the diaries with me, says bitterly, "The mill don't care what day it is." She resented it when Jinx, her husband, had to report to the Irvin Works on holidays, even though it meant extra pay. "How come you didn't hate shifts like I did, Mom?" she asks.

Consistent with the *persona* of her diaries, Ruth says, "I was so much in love with your father that I didn't care."

For twenty-five years, Jinx worked swing shifts, and Sandy felt like a single mother. "He was never here when I wanted him to be and we couldn't plan anything unless there was a layoff or strike, which wasn't the best thing either," Sandy says. "And if the kids heard about a mill accident on TV they always panicked."

Twelve years ago Sandy didn't see anything positive about mill life, except the money. But now she's grateful that the Irvin Works still operates, and wishes Jinx weren't around the house as much. Since he now works only day turn and Sandy has a part-time job in a hardware store, she can't clean at night the way she used to because "Jinx is on the couch at 8 watching television."

Few men I talked with acknowledged how working shifts affected their wives and families. Joe Havrilla, 88, and I talked in the Homestead Library, not far from where a portrait of Andrew Carnegie watches over the return desk. A retired "white hat" for over twenty years, Havrilla spent time with me before going off to bowl in an AARP league. As a young man with a wife and four children, he had worked turns. "The mother was home all the time. Shifts didn't mean anything to her," he says, depersonalizing his wife as he answers my questions about how his family accommodated his shifts. "She prepared her meals according to the husband's working and children going to school. And they came home from school for lunch because there weren't cafeterias in those early days."

"It didn't make any difference what shift I worked. No shift was hard for me," Havrilla claims. Then the afterthought: ". . . maybe hard for my wife because she had to take care of everything, see the kids off to school. But she drove a car and took the kids wherever they had to go," he told me.

Raymond Stevens, 86, was the rare ex-steelworker to say "women worked in horrible conditions but weren't appreciated." Stevens' eyes were sad as he talked with me at an aluminum table at a meeting for former steelworkers in a basement room of the Homestead Elks. "When I go to Florida now and look at the winter sky at night, I get tears in my eyes at what my mother would think. How she worked around the clock, went without food and raised four children through strikes," Stevens says. Overhearing our conversation, another steelworker has little patience, and bullies: "Don't listen to him. He lies like a Russian pimp."

Typically, steelworkers do not draw connections between the quality of their family life and the mill schedule. They deflect any conversation about how their wives kept their homes running smoothly. When I asked Jim Boland what it was like working shifts with a family, he said, "She handled the kids as far as I know."

Donald Gregor is an anomaly. He and his wife Pat often spent their savings because he worked at locally owned plants where strikes and layoffs were common. They raised eight children in a small home in a wooded area outside Pittsburgh, where they lived off the land, killed rabbits and small game, and canned vegetables for the winter months. After their youngest child started school in 1966, Donald insisted that Pat, at age 41, enroll as a freshman at California University in California, Pennsylvania so that she could provide for herself and the children in case of his death or permanent injury. Besides that, he thought she was smart and deserved an education.

"The men at work made it rough for him," Pat says. "They just couldn't believe sending daughters to college because they'd 'just get married,' but for a wife to go was beyond their belief. They kept telling him I'd leave him and the kids, and go off somewhere."

Pat describes Donald, now deceased, as a bright, wonderful man, who "read everything. Without him and the support of the kids, I wouldn't have been able to do it." After completing a bachelor's degree in 1966, she earned a master's degree as a reading specialist and taught in elementary school.

Another steelworker recognizing the burdens of a mill wife is Martin Conners, but he didn't know how to make things better. He still laments missing his son's First Communion because of having to work. "I had a rotten boss who didn't like you to take days off. I used to work Sundays all the time and that's when first communions were," Conners explains. "I have pictures but I didn't get to see it."

Working shifts contributed to the breakup of his marriage, Conners thinks. "But mostly it was because of working 4 to midnight for a long stint. I couldn't be home to help my kids with their homework, or do much of anything with them. After a while my wife figured out, 'What do I need you for? You're not here most of the time.'"

Adele Vamos, 50, says missing her father was the worst part of being a mill kid. "Hearing the river foghorns and the clanging of the mills at night would remind me that he was down there. The only times you really saw your dad was the week he worked daylight from 8 to 4. Other times you had to be real quiet because he was sleeping. Being quiet, oh, that was hard. But the men were so tired. They were never able to develop a good sleeping regimen because of their schedules."

Memories of shifts are individual and often nostalgic. Bedroom windows were usually darkened by green or maroon roller shades so that men working night turn could sleep during the day.

When Bonnie Harvey, one of six children, was growing up, her grandfather, a steelworker, lived with her family. "Our house was the gathering spot on the street, and yet we couldn't bounce a ball on the porch because 'Pap's going to work tonight,'" her mother would scold.

Walking back to school after eating lunch at home during the austere days of World War II, the five little Miller sisters liked looking through the big windows of the bustling barrooms that lined Carson Street, near the Jones & Laughlin plant on Pittsburgh's South Side. "I can still see the men standing at the bar, cracking hardboiled eggs, and those bottles of pigs' feet lined up," Millie Carlino says to me, her four sisters and brother Elmer, as we sit around her dining room table. "We were proud that this was our neighborhood, our home," they all agree. "It was a comfortable feeling. We were more afraid of the Catholic kids who'd poke us in the back when we passed their school than we ever were of any steelworker."

As a teenager, Mary Jo Bensasi, 42, liked driving the family car to pick up her father when he worked on weekends. A lot of kids did that," Mary Jo says. "It was just a fact of life. If we were at a party, we just left and drove to the mill. It's the way things were, and we didn't feel we were missing anything or giving anything up."

When their children were old enough to leave alone at midnight, Helen Havrilla, now 87, was glad to save her husband a long walk home, although she kept a baseball bat beside her on the passenger seat in case someone jumped her car while she was alone in it. "It was a peaceful time to talk and be together," she says.

Surprising her husband after his midnight shift was a favorite part of Bev Lucanish's day. "I'd wake the kids and put them in the car, then we'd stop and get pizza. It was midnight, but it was nice—real nice to be together."

A mill wife for forty years and now a widow for seven, Hazel Jackson still cannot bear to sit alone on her front porch where she and her husband Frank used to talk and eat sandwiches of melted cheese and fried onions when he got home at midnight. "It was a sandwich his mother concocted, and so I learned how to make them, and we ate them together," Hazel smiles. "We'd just sit on the porch and watch the traffic go by because we lived on a busy corner and men were still driving home from the mill."

As Hazel reminisces, her daughter, Jan McSorley, listens, remembering the odor of frying onions wafting up to the second-floor bedrooms. "When I smelled the onions and cheese, I knew Dad was home and everything was all right," she adds.

Chapter 5

❦

Women's Work
You buy . . . you cook . . . you donate.

A steelworker's wife had little variation in the days, months and years of her life. On Mondays, she washed, and on Tuesdays, she ironed. On Wednesdays, she paid the bills at the bank because payday was Tuesday. On Saturday, she cleaned for Sunday visitors. And on Sundays, she cooked and served. Children hated coming home from school on Mondays because wet clothes would be strung across the first floor, and the house would reek of Fels Naptha soap.

Washing, ironing, scrubbing and cooking filled a mill wife's day because her work was crucial to the family's stability, and also because most steelworkers believed that women belonged in the home.

This routine lasted from the beginning of the twentieth century until long after the publication in 1963 of Betty Friedan's *The Feminine Mystique* motivated many women to evaluate their domestic lives and wake up to personal ambition. Only in retrospect do mill wives appreciate how they wore themselves out performing endless chores and worrying about their husbands' safety.

"Cooking and cleaning was all I ever did," Helen Havrilla, the mother of six children, told me across tea and pastries at her daughter-in-law's dining room table. "Whatever Steve's schedule, I always had to work around it. And the work never got easier because it was always the same; you were always with children," she explains. "You never heard of babysitters. After dinner, women would sit outside and crochet in the evenings. I'd embroider pillowcases, doilies, even towels. We'd talk."

Helen spoke tentatively at first, convinced that she had nothing interesting to tell me. But by the end of our conversation, she talked with confidence, empowered, I think, by hearing her own voice describe what it was like to grow up as the daughter and wife of steelworkers.

She is the last of a generation of Steel Valley pioneers. When she was born in 1916, her parents were living in a strange new world, for her father had left poverty in Slovakia to work at the Homestead plant. With handmade tools carried from the "old country," Slovak friends helped him build a family home high above Homestead, where cherry trees and vegetables could flourish away from the mill's red dust. "The Slovak people were handy and adept at survival, but they were fearful and stayed together and helped each other," remarks Nick Havrilla, Helen's oldest son, who remembers his grandfather.

As a child, Helen canned pickles, beets and tomatoes for the winter with her mother's friends and their children. "The children always worked and played at the same time. I enjoyed all that, especially Sunday afternoons when we'd walk, sometimes long distances, to each other's homes. We'd trade vegetables, eggs and chickens. The women would quilt and the little girls would thread their needles."

Helen considers herself fortunate to have graduated from high school because her sister had to stay home to help their mother "cook, put up, bake. That was expected of girls in families," she remarks. But Helen's opportunities weren't much different. She was employed as a domestic/cook and she turned over her weekly salary to her parents.

Helen met her husband Stephen through the family for whom she worked. He made deliveries for the florist shop they owned and often dropped off groceries for Helen at the kitchen door. Couples seldom married outside their ethnic group for fear of being ostracized by their families, but Stephen's parents were also from Slovakia, so they were a great match. While they dated, he started working at the Homestead plant and Helen got a new job as a file clerk at Mercy Hospital.

"It was tough for me to give up working," Helen says softly, "but that was expected after you got married." To save money, the newlyweds lived with her parents for two years. Helen and her mother navigated the same kitchen at different times because the two men seldom worked the same shift. "I just kept up like I had before. When Steve came home from the mill I had to feed him, take care of his clothes." Helen rubbed his overalls with lard to get out the grease.

As their family grew, Helen looked forward to spending a week at a camp outside of Pittsburgh that U. S. Steel provided each summer for mill kids and their mothers. There were swimming pools, sports, games, a wishing tree and counselors to look after the kids. "We didn't have to cook. The mothers relaxed. This is when I had a vacation. I wanted a tan," Helen confides.

The kitchen is the central image when Steel Valley women connect with memories of their mothers. For Helen, as for other wives, there was no end to cooking and baking, especially on Sundays. After attending early Mass, she would start her chicken soup by making homemade noodles. Like many other women in the Steel Valley, she learned to cook the way her mother-in-law did. "I had to make all the foods he had had at home," Helen says. "And I had to make the same kind of noodles. All them noodles! I wouldn't want to do it anymore. I'd cook all afternoon. Soup and noodles for supper! We never measured in those days. Made our own dough. You had to guess how much this or that. There was always flour to work on with a rolling pin or your fingers. Every day was much the same."

By the end of our conversation, Helen was pretty feisty. "The father was always boss," she said. "You had to get used to that. But at least he worked. There were strikes and no one paid you then. I've tried to shut out from my mind what strikes were like. But families traded clothes and helped each other."

Besides cooking and cleaning at home, Helen volunteered in the cafeteria of her children's school, sold chances to raise money for the church, and prepared food for parish picnics. Succinctly, and without a smile, she finally summed up the life of a steelworker's wife: "You buy . . . you cook . . . you donate."

Hundreds of other Steel Valley women were also lonely in their kitchens but lacked the advantage of being born in the United States and speaking English. Immigrant wives arriving at the depots of mill towns wore signs around their necks to identify their native language. They were greeted in pidgin Polish, Slovak, Hungarian and Russian by volunteers like Dorothy Miller, whose parents' native tongue was Rumanian.

Miller's five daughters recalled how fascinated they were to hear their mother—the daughter and wife of steelworkers—speak other languages. They always thought she was an "important person" in Pittsburgh's South Side because of the many women who knocked at their door, depending upon her for help because she could communicate in so many languages, including Serbian and Croatian. "Women had problems with their husbands. They'd move out and not leave any money for the family. Mom knew women were being treated like second-class citizens, and she tried to explain and interpret things for them," says Dorothy's daughter, Millie Carlino.

Even when their husbands preceded them from Europe and met them at the train station, the transition from Europe to the Steel Valley was daunting for an immigrant woman.

Julia Hrika and her three children arrived in Homestead in 1929 from Slovakia, seven years after her husband. Because he had become a United States citizen, his small family was able to bypass the procedures of Ellis Island and travel directly to Pittsburgh. But Julia's future was not as easy as her arrival.

Her daughter Mary Hrika Soncini, now 80, was moved to tears as she and her brother John, 82, talked about their mother's struggles, which began in Slovakia, where Julia's father owned acres of farmland and a brick house that is still standing. "He had money and influence," Mary says. "He educated two sons to be physicians, but didn't believe in educating women," and had no intention of bequeathing any property to Julia after she married John Hrika, whom he considered to be a pauper.

Without any special skills, Hrika left Slovakia in 1922, and "ended up working in a steel mill," his son John says. After seven years of receiving little money from her husband and having no hope of an inheritance from her father, Julia became "aggressive," John remembers, and said, "'We're going to go [to America].' Her family was probably holding her back from leaving earlier," he speculates. But arriving in Homestead in 1929 was bad timing.

During the Depression, steelworkers were seldom called to work more than one or two days a month. Unemployed men passed time by playing cards in the courtyards of the Ward, surrounded by children, while their wives earned 75 cents a day cleaning houses. "My grandfather had people working for him, and now my mother is in this country as a servant," says Mary. "So many times I saw her cry. It still hurts me about her."

To save the 10-cent trolley fare, Julia walked miles from her home in the Ward,

67

crossing a long bridge over the Monongahela River and climbing a three-mile hill to an affluent neighborhood where she cleaned for an attorney's family. She cut through backyards, trying to beat the trolley, to and from work. In the evenings, she washed dishes by hand at a popular Homestead restaurant. Mary often joined her mother to peel potatoes and dry the dishes.

Although Mary and John picked up English by playing with other children, wives of steelworkers had few opportunities to learn it. Julia, however, arranged for a teacher to give English lessons to a group of women in her kitchen. "She was always trying to improve her life, but if things had been different, I'm sure she would have been a nurse or doctor," Mary says. "She died young, at 62, because of all the stress and hard work."

And after a week of hard work, wives wanted to relax with friends who spoke the same language. "Women had the sense of mind to relax on Sundays and come together," claims Martha Sloan, sixty-nine. As the youngest child in her family, Martha went everywhere with her mother, who spoke only Slovakian. "Sunday was church, was rest time. You didn't gad about and shop like today." After a big noon meal, Martha and her parents went with other families to a park, where the women talked and danced to gypsy orchestras while the men played pinochle and drank homemade wine and moonshine. "The women talked about who was getting married, and what they were baking for the wedding. A wedding took three days and women baked a whole week prior to it," Martha explains.

Funerals also provided female companionship. "The person was laid out in the home and the women would spend three days at the house, baking, cooking and praying while the men played cards," Martha tells me. Neither her mother nor father learned to speak English, and Martha spoke Slovak until she started first grade.

Within the small town of Rankin, where nationality groups chose to live together on certain streets, women with the same ethnic backgrounds met after dinner in the alleys and courtyards of their row houses to crochet, knit and exchange recipes. Visiting Braddock and Rankin during the strike of 1919, labor historian Mary Heaton Vorse described Slovak and Croatian women in "squalid courtyards" singing while weaving "bright colored rugs," and nodding in "village fashion as I pass." From the time Anne Pcholinsky was a little girl in Rankin over sixty-five years ago, she remembers women, in clean housedresses, arranging kitchen chairs in circles behind their homes, enjoying a respite after the dishes were put away. "But, you know, it was great for them because they relieved so much of their tension. Almost like group therapy." While the women wanted their children to learn English, they spoke to each other with the comfort of their European languages. A common topic of conversation was the pressure they felt from relatives in Europe who kept asking them to send money. "They always felt our streets were paved with gold and couldn't understand we didn't have anything to spare," said Helen Havrilla. "After a while you just had to break away from them."

Women also socialized at church. Most Steel Valley towns had numerous ethnic churches, often across the street from each other. At St. Michael's Orthodox Church in Rankin, women took turns baking the bread for Communion. "Oh, God, how those women lived," Anne exclaims. "I can almost place where they sat in church. This one sat there; that one sat there. Some of them wore babushkas, but for church on Sunday morning, they'd dress up with pretty little hats and plain black coats. Sunday services were like the beginning of the week. And if you didn't go, they thought something's going to happen to you. Then they'd go home to see who would come to visit and eat the things they'd baked on Saturday. People dropping in—that was the entertainment," Anne's eyes grow shiny as she conjures the images.

About the only place mill wives went besides church was the grocery store. They shopped easily in neighborhood markets because owners knew key words in numerous languages. Jewish shopkeepers were known for switching from Polish to Russian to Hungarian to Italian, depending upon the customer. "The Jewish businessmen catered to the mill wives," says Martha Sloan, remembering how her mother spoke only Slovak, bought from the "Jewish huckster, the Jewish baker, and there was a Jewish guy that fixed umbrellas and sharpened knives. A Jewish guy at the end of the road sold shoes, curtains, dresses and material. That's the way it was and my mother had no real need to speak English."

Food bills were quickly tallied on paper bags and not charged until the end of the month. If a bill was questioned, mothers blamed the store, not themselves, their children told me.

Very aware of the family budget, immigrant women often knew numbers before letters. Betty Esper, the mayor of Homestead, has lived in the same neighborhood, once an enclave for Syrians, all of her life. She describes her Syrian mother as a "strictly immigrant type of lady. Her job was to cook, clean, wash clothes and be a great mother. I guess I never appreciated her until, like we all do, until after. She couldn't read or write, but we still keep a tablet where she might have been practicing. I always say she was the first person that brought in dial-by-number. She couldn't read, so she didn't know to dial the letters that used to start phone numbers. We'd just say dial 461-1405. If you told her to dial MO, she'd say huh?"

A mother's style and sense of ceremony, even in poverty, could ease the real pressures in a steelworker's family. For example, Jane Bodnar's mother never complained and made the best of it when Jane's father was seriously injured at Homestead by a crane "with a big hook" that grazed his back and kidney. From then on, he had only menial jobs in the mill, but she "cleaned houses to help out."

One of six children, Jane cherished the simple pleasures of growing up in a row house in the Ward, where her family managed with two bedrooms. When the Ward was demolished for the expansion of the Homestead Works at the start of World War II, the family moved to a larger home in a project. "It meant that Mom had more room to move around, but also that she did more cooking and baking," Jane says. "But if you could just see our happiness at night when we were all together, especially on holidays. All the odors coming from the kitchen, and the house smelling so clean. By the time we sat down, everything was so exciting. And yet it wasn't that much. Just family life and togetherness."

But not all women were resigned to the simple pleasures of a steelworker's family, especially if they did not grow up in one.

Isabel and Eugene Shatlock are happy to talk about his mother Mae, whose father owned a butcher shop in Erie, Pennsylvania. "They were a little bit more affluent than the Shatlocks of Homestead," Eugene adds about his mother's family. But Isabel is bursting to say more. "Mae wore a red outfit, a long skirt with a slit, the first time she met her mother-in-law," which would have been around 1920. "She couldn't get over that Mae wasn't wearing long underwear, and that her stockings were showing. Mae said her in-laws looked at her as if she was kind of flashing, you know," Isabel chuckles.

Once Mae and Paul Shatlock married and moved in with his parents, "Mae pressured my father-in-law to put a bathroom in. So the poor man put plumbing in the house for her," Isabel shakes her head as if she wouldn't have made such demands herself.

Steelworkers living in the Ward added small bathrooms underneath the outdoor steps that led into the sides of their houses. They're called "Pittsburgh bathrooms" because men dirty and sweaty from working their shift could go directly into the bathroom without entering the house.

But a Pittsburgh bathroom was not the answer for Mae. "She returned to Erie because she just couldn't get used to Homestead. She felt it was primitive compared to Erie, where her family had a washing machine." (Women in the Ward washed clothes by hand on scrub boards.) "Paul went to Erie and brought her back," Isabel says simply.

Isabel listened to Mae's stories and watched her household routine when she and Eugene lived with his parents for a few months after he returned from World War II, and long after Paul and Mae had left the Ward.

"She did everything," marvels Isabel, one of six daughters of a physician from Pittsburgh. "And his father came home for lunch every day. He was thin so she baked a lot for him. Every year she either washed the walls or painted because of all the soot. And that was the routine. She was some woman!"

Like Isabel Shatlock, others were eager to tell me about plucky women in the Steel Valley whose lives they still wonder about.

For example, Lorraine Novak's grandmother, Mary Meyer, made hats "for fancy people" in Pittsburgh. "She was classy. I know her mother wrote poetry. My grandfather married her and I have the bill where he paid for a buggy to bring her to Duquesne from Pittsburgh. She must have had culture shock when she got here," Lorraine frowns.

By contrast, Lorraine's in-laws, Anna and Nick, met at a dance in Duquesne and when they decided to marry, "Baba sent two men to McKeesport where Nick's intended lived to carry all her luggage. But she only had a brown paper bag with a dress change in it and a pair of stockings. We've always laughed that two men carried the bag back."

The new bride immediately went to work helping her husband's parents run the U. S. Steel "camps" located in Duquesne "below the tracks," where newly arrived steelworkers from Europe without families slept and ate. Anna and her mother-in-law Sara prepared meals for as many as fifty men around the mill's shifts, laundered their clothes and cleaned out spittoons. Bedsheets were not changed regularly, for as one man left for work, another hopped into his still-warm bed.

Running the camps "was a good living during the Depression," Lorraine says. "The women did everything. Made their own whiskey. Probably ran numbers. And Grandpap never worked a day in his life. Sara married him in Europe. She was fifteen, he was fourteen. And he sat and watched her build a house. He worked in the steel mill three months and got a pension."

After the camps closed, Anna had a job in a chocolate factory and then in the Duquesne Works during World War II, making bullets. "It was never work that was too hard for her. I never heard her complain about the steel mill. But I remember she wasn't happy with the smell of the chocolate factory," Lorraine says.

To make ends meet, other churchgoing, Godfearing, hardworking women, like Lorraine's relatives, were often into gambling and bathtub gin. One woman who was a child during the Depression has vivid images of steelworkers coming in and out of her grandmother's kitchen, where she ran a continuous poker game for low stakes. Alex Savo, a baby during Prohibition, was a decoy in his buggy, sitting atop blankets and bottles of moonshine, as his mother and brother made deliveries to speakeasies in and about Homestead. Another woman told me that her mother-in-law "made hootch and put it in the carriage under the baby. Those were the things women did to help the family income."

The early mill wives' ability to confront change and uncertainty is a legacy that their female relatives want to perpetuate. For example, Anna Marie Sninsky has written and illustrated *Potatoes Save Mary,* a little book about her mother-in-law that she reads to elementary school children. Mary Gaulden, born in Shariska, Slovakia, in 1893, came to America by herself at the age of thirteen to join her parents in Grassflat, Pennsylvania. When Mary was seasick, a Slovakian cook promised to keep Mary well if she would peel potatoes for her. "Mary for weeks eats potatoes . . . comes to Homestead to work in a restaurant. Cooks potatoes . . . marries John Sninsky, bears nine children and cooks more potatoes," Anna Marie reads. She uses the book to encourage children to discover traits of fortitude and forbearance in women in their own families.

I talked with one young woman who filters her own experiences through the history of her immigrant grandmothers, one who died before she was even born.

"What I've always wondered about," says Mary Cvetan, 38, is the type of woman who left the old country, and got on a boat to come to this new experience. Were they adventurous, pioneering types by nature or didn't they have a choice? Or was life so tentative?" Looking at me intensely, Mary expects no answers to her question.

Antonia Cvetan, the grandmother Mary knew, was academically gifted. She finished the equivalent of ninth grade in Yugoslavia, and was on track to be a teacher until her parents needed her to work on their farm. At some point, Mary recalls, she was employed as a nanny for a wealthy family and traveled with them to Italy. "So how does a person go from living in Europe in fresh air, in the countryside, and with some taste of a cultured life, and get stuck in Braddock, which is sooty, dirty and smoky, and wash my grandfather's mill clothes by hand?"

During Mary's freshman year at Carlow College, now University, her grandmother died. She was so proud of Mary that she left her all that she had, a meager bequest but big enough to help Mary buy a car after graduation. Antonia was proud of her granddaughter not because she was smart and had won a writing scholarship, but because Mary had pursued an opportunity to get ahead.

Mary feels close to her grandmothers because of the values she received from them by pondering their lives. "You see what's possible if you look at the examples right in front of you. When I hear about my grandmother living on a farm with pigs, that seems like another planet because I'm on the Internet eighteen hours a day struggling to build up my advertising and marketing business. I'm not tilling the soil for dinner. But it's really not another planet. It's all about risk and optimism and hard work."

Chapter 6

Women Who Did Men's Work

I was just glad to have a little chance to know what it was like.

Once they settled in the Steel Valley, mill wives seldom left. If they felt stifled by domestic routine, creativity was their ticket out.

Women had their tricks for facing everyday life—lard to remove grease from workmen's clothes, barley soup as nature's perfect food for a new mother, coal ashes for brushing teeth—but also remedies for ailments and skill in setting bones.

Some women were held in awe for their ability to heal illnesses, rashes and even fractures. Stories of their curative powers have qualities of legend for they contain elements of mystery and often superstition.

Every Monday, Anna Vasko boiled large kettles of water to wash her family's clothes, and spent hours wringing them by hand. She didn't have magic solutions for avoiding the laundry, but once finished, she became the "local pharmacist," and withdrew to her "office" on the sun porch, where she saw patients all hours of the day and night. "Just go see Annya, go see Annya, she'll take care of you," her daughter, Martha Sloan, imitates the people of the neighborhood.

Anna made poultices from rags and concocted medicines from herbs she gathered from her garden, but only after midnight. She had separate formulas for treating arthritis, cuts or sore throats. To cure rashes, she compounded gels and creams on the kitchen stove. She smeared salve on "scratchy leaves" that she wrapped around the swollen legs of men who probably had gout, Martha remembers.

Spearmint was Anna's herb of choice because of its versatility. "If you stayed home from school with a bellyache, she cooked it with scrambled eggs or broth," Martha says, pointing to a pot of spearmint she keeps in her kitchen window.

Two of Martha's four children are now pharmacists.

In the middle of telling me about his mother who "fixed more arms and legs than all four of the doctors in this town [Rankin] put together," Charles Belevek, 89, suddenly stops, and reconsiders. "Well, there's nobody can do anything about that now anyway because, you know, she's gone; that's practicing without a license. Today, in this age, you'd go to jail for that."

Adults and children came to his mother with dislocated and broken limbs, Belevek is proud to say. "But no one knows, you understand, how she did it." Returning home from school in the afternoon, he'd see kids leaving the house with wrapped arms or legs, but "I never seen her in operation, only when I got hurt."

Teetering on a stool at the Rankin Borough Building where he answers the telephone, Belevek risks his limbs again, trying to recreate how, as a boy, he had bent his hand backwards from the wrist, from a fall. "So what she did, she was washing walls at the time, she told me to sit in the chair. Then she grabbed my arm and put her leg up against my chest and pulled it. Snapped it back into position." Finally, she bathed his arm in vinegar and water, and wrapped it with a piece of flour sack from the local baker. Belevek wiggles his hand to show me, that after all these years, it still works fine.

When Lorraine Novak's grandfather John, nicknamed Sonny, married Mary Meyer, she became known as Sonny's Mary. Nonetheless, Mary developed her own identity as a healer in Duquesne, after moving from Pittsburgh, where she made hats. "She wasn't a nurse, but she took care of everybody in the neighborhood," Lorraine says. "Anybody that got hurt had to come to Sonny's Mary for treatment."

Her most famous cure occurred when Sonny suffered a compound fracture from falling off scaffolding while helping to build a house. "Doctors wanted to take his leg off," recalls Lorraine, "but my grandmother said absolutely not. I'll save that leg. She treated it, and she did save it. He had a limp until he passed away, but otherwise he never had any trouble," Lorraine marvels.

All the neighborhood kids liked to play in Sonny Mary's yard because she gave them huge slices of her homemade bread smothered with jelly. In case of injury, parents were glad that she was nearby. Late one afternoon, when telling kids it was time to head home, she spotted a twelve-year-old boy, with a cast on his leg, sitting on the steps. Curious about his injury, she detected an odor coming from the cast, and told his parents to have it removed. "She saved that kid's leg," Lorraine says, "because it was already decaying."

Not all women who practiced the art of healing had the nascent medical knowledge of Sonny's Mary. To bring about cures, some women invented rituals. Getting rid of headaches was one mother's specialty. Her octogenarian son, preferring not to be named, remembers her pouring holy water from their church into a glass, then striking a wooden match, and putting it into a glass. If the match submerged, it told her one thing, and if it floated, it told her something else. "Whatever she did from there on in, I don't know, but she'd take this water and wipe my head with it, and the fever would go away. She was gifted," he told me.

Old-timers often thought illness was the result of an enemy casting an "evil eye." If one of Dorothy Miller's five daughters were sick and home from school, they remember she would hold a wooden clothespin over a pot of vigorously boiling water. When the clothespin became hot as an ingot, she'd zing it into the pot and say a few prayers to dispel the curse. The sisters—Millie Carlino, Mary Lou Collinger, Dorothy Hines, Esther Miller and Ellen Dale Slinsky—laugh together, uncertain whether their mother was psychologically astute or naively superstitious, because by morning they generally felt better.

"Steelworkers' wives didn't think they were really working, even if they were taking care of ten children because they followed the same routine, day in and day out," says Bonnie Harvey, CEO of the Carnegie Library of Homestead. Her own mother, Eileen O'Leary Boyle, an artist, was an exception. She tested pottery clay in the oven, soaked paint brushes on the kitchen table, couldn't bake and served "terrible chop suey for dinner. Growing up with a nontraditional mother had its challenges," Bonnie laughs. "I often felt like an outsider among my friends. This community is very slow to change."

Until the last decade, women were prohibited from using the Homestead Library's gym after 9 A.M. or the swimming pool at the same time as men. "Women swim crooked," men told Harvey.

The steelworkers' message to women until World War II was stay in your place and out of the way. It was the gutsy woman who defied the unwritten rule and an unusual man who tolerated his wife's employment, especially if both husband and wife had to hold jobs that involved working shifts.

"My husband was different for a Slovak man, because they always want to be boss," says Anna Mae Vamos, 79. "It's not fifty-fifty. They want power over you. But that didn't happen with us. I just did my thing, and he didn't mind that I worked all those years."

For forty-five years, Anna Mae was the star waitress at H & H, a 24-hour restaurant on Homestead's bustling Eighth Avenue, while her husband, Stephen, worked shifts at the Homestead plant. "He knew I loved waitress work and he never says to me *quit*. I quit on my own when I was fifty-seven. But then he was on pension and the mill was down. He was mad that I quit. He says, 'Why don't you go to work? Get a job, hon.'"

Anna Mae and her daughter Adele, 50, talk with me at Anna Mae's kitchen table, where mushrooms are drying over the sink in preparation for a special soup on Christmas Eve. Anna Mae talks of the "good old days" when she and Steve tried to balance their work schedules, but Adele says the kids were burdened.

Adele, the oldest of four young children, looked after her siblings with the help of her grandmother, Baba Vamos, who lived in a little house in their narrow backyard. "If we were lonely or had an emergency, we always had the security that Baba was there," Adele says while pulling back the kitchen curtain so that I can see how close the houses are.

"We used to call Mom a lot when she was at the restaurant, and now that I'm a mother, I realize how hard that must have been for her," Adele says. Their calls were persistent around dinner, a hectic time for any waitress. "But," Anna Mae interrupts, "that's when Adele had her hands full. She had to start supper and make sure the kids were bathed." Unless Anna Mae was able to catch an early bus or a ride home, the children didn't get to see either parent very much.

Adele never depended on her father being home to help. "Like most men during those years, he went out after work and stayed out. But if he did come home, I still made the dinner or my grandmother would bring over pots of soup or stew." As a child, Adele managed the family food budget through two strikes and two layoffs. "They were tough times," she says. "I can remember going to the Whitaker School to pick up cheese and powdered milk subsidies. But as the main cook here, I made that last a long time."

After Adele says good-bye and leaves for home, her mother cries out at the kitchen table, "Oh, we hated to leave them, but we had to. We had to work to live to eat. . . . "

When a steelworker finally accepted that his wife could be a wage earner, her household responsibilities shifted to other women in the family. In this new arrangement, husbands gained freedom and overworked wives harbored guilt.

"I always claimed our father was the first liberated man," says Millie Carlino, a daughter of Dorothy Miller, an elected member of the local Democratic committee for forty years and an active participant in Roosevelt's New Deal Club. "Mom had political meetings at the house, but Dad never interfered. She was up front and he was always in the background, but they were equals," says Millie, one of their nine children.

Dorothy Miller built a loyal political base by helping immigrant women when they first arrived at the depot on Pittsburgh's South Side. Because she had an ear for languages, these women often wanted her with them in childbirth, to translate their wishes to the doctor. Millie and her sisters speculate that their mother eventually entered politics to increase job options for their father, who was often laid off from Jones & Laughlin because of strikes. After he became a member of the electricians' union and got a city job, the Miller family gained financial security. "All our lives we heard, 'If you're screwy, vote for Dewey,'" Millie says.

As an elected delegate to the Pennsylvania Constitutional Convention in 1967-68, Miller became friends with James A. Michener, the Pulitzer Prize-winning novelist, who served as Secretary to the Convention, a post he considered the "most important political role" of his life. For each of Miller's children, he autographed one of his novels. He inscribed *The Source*:

> *To Ellen Dale Slinsky, whose lovely mother is a dear friend.*
> *Shalom,*
> *James A. Michener*

"When Daddy died in 1958, Mommy got a job—a *man's job*—the sisters emphasize. The mayor of Pittsburgh, David L. Lawrence, offered her a position in the Bureau of Building Permits. When she said she was worried that she didn't know how to figure building specifications, Lawrence told her, "You'll learn." And she did. For decades, Dorothy Miller had political clout, but that job was the first where she earned a salary.

Less aggressive women than she had crossed over into male jobs much earlier. For example, Pat French talks about her mother, Diana Jordanoff Kaye. Born in Bulgaria in 1901, Diana married Zlaty Jordanoff, who left home after the first Balkan War, but returned to Bulgaria after fifteen years in the United States to find a wife.

"Diana was the darling of the whole village," Pat says, "and so the powers that be—my mother's grandparents, the priest, and others—decided that she should be the one to marry this American."

Within two months she married Zlaty and set sail for America, where he was a railroad worker in New Castle. Starved for Bulgarian friends, they moved to Homestead, where he became a partner in a grocery store that he later lost during the Depression. The couple rented rooms in their apartment to two Bulgarian steelworkers, who stayed with them for seventeen years. "My mother took care of everything," Pat says, "and also worked at the Bulgarian Center where she made meals for all those Bulgarian bachelors that hung around."

By this time, Pat was in first grade, and learning English. "None of the people around the club knew English, but my mother started to pick it up from me, and decided to go to work. That was unheard of for an immigrant woman who didn't speak English," Pat stresses, "but she got a job at the Amos Supermarket working the cash register. Her English was horrible, but she was excellent in math."

Next, Diana wanted to drive, and Pat's father said flatly, "Women don't drive cars." But she got a friend to teach her, passed the test, and "waved her driver's license in my father's face," Pat says proudly.

During World War II, Diana was one of the first women hired in the mill, at $6.48 a day. "Zlaty was ashamed that our people would see me doing that kind of work," Diana said in an interview for *Out of This Kitchen* shortly before her death in 1993.

"That was the turning point," says Martha Sloan, 69, the daughter of a steelworker and a savvy observer of life in the Steel Valley. "Until then, women were more backward, more intimidated because men were the bosses. None of my women relatives ever worked, but when the mills got short-handed, a couple of my aunts got good jobs and made good money. 'I wear a steel hat. I run a crane.' Boy, how their attitudes changed!"

Women accounted for less than one percent of the workforce in the steel industry between 1910 and 1930, just a decade before the war. One of them, Ruth Haas, 89, with a fresh perm, white slacks and pink sleeveless top, is excited to be at her daughter's kitchen table, slicing supermarket coffeecake, telling me about her job in the Shenango Mill, New Castle, Pennsylvania.

After high school graduation, Ruth joined the "tin line" at the mill, where her mother was a veteran of twenty years. "Lines of women up and down, all did the same thing. We sorted tin. Put the primes in one pile and the seconds in the other pile," Ruth's hands move as if squaring off stacks. "If they weren't perfect, we erased them and made them a prime." Ruth loved her job because of the money— "10 cents an hour was good."

Women were thought to have special talent for sorting tin because of their supposed patience, sharp eyesight and attention to detail. But outside of the tin line, management and labor agreed that a steel plant was not a place for women. Steel mills were fueled by male labor because of tough-minded white hats, dangerous conditions and ingrained Old World attitudes about roles suitable for women. In a study titled "The Problem Every Supervisor Dreads: Women Workers at the U. S. Steel, Duquesne Works during World War II," Jim Rose documents a statement by a union worker at a meeting of USWA Local 1256 in 1942, arguing against teaching women to operate cranes, because their "place is in the home to raise our next generation of children."

A manager was willing to risk the health of workers rather than admit nurses to the Jones & Laughlin plant: "The mill is too dangerous," Rose quotes him as saying. "We have two nurses and it would be a great help to them in treating accidents if they knew something of the processes at which the men had been injured, but we simply cannot let them in."

Women were even shut out of office jobs in Steel Valley mills, where men held the monopoly on clerical positions at a time when women staffed corporate offices in the city of Pittsburgh.

One old-timer told me that men were free to "pee whenever, wherever they wanted" before the age of women in the mills. But the demands of World War II forced changes in attitudes about women in industrial jobs. Suddenly it became "natural" and patriotic for women to meet the heavy demands of labor and "Rosie the Riveter" with her acetylene torch and flexed muscle became the emblem for the six million women joining the workforce. In August 1943, *Newsweek* reported Rosie "in the shipyards, lumber mills, steel mills, foundries. [Women] are welders, electricians, mechanics, and even boilermakers. They operate streetcars, buses, cranes, and tractors. Women engineers are working in the drafting room and women physicists and chemists in the great industrial laboratories."

Overnight, the steel industry gave women a bigger role in office management and on the production floor. They went from polishing tin by hand, as Ruth Haas had done, to operating heavy equipment. And most of them loved their new challenges.

When I arrived at the home of Urelia "Rickie" Filipos, she couldn't wait to show me her crane operator's license, dated July 17, 1944. At the age of 81, she'd go back to her old job "in a minute. It was the best job I ever had."

Filipos was a clerk at the Main Gate of Homestead Steel when a notice circulated for crane operators. She didn't hesitate to apply. She was always interested in how machinery worked, but had never dreamed of an opportunity to run it. A diminutive woman with yellow hair in bangs and radiant blue eyes, she describes her hard-hat job with feminine imagery. "Getting the hook into the right place was like threading a needle. I hauled steel from one place to another, and the men were always glad to see me. They knew I was very careful and never had an accident," she says with irrepressible pride.

Rickie liked her job too much to care which shift she worked or how cold she felt in the winds blowing into the mill from across the Monongahela River. "I liked the feel of controlling the equipment and knowing how the machine operated," she says, moving her fists back and forth as if maneuvering levers. "But after the war, I just got married, and that was that."

Rickie walked me to the door with one more thing to say. "Anytime I'm at the Waterfront [the huge shopping center where the Homestead plant used to be] I always look over to where I drove the crane and feel so bad it's no longer there."

A sense of loss permeated all my conversations with ex-Rosies. Back then, the possibility of staying at work in the mill or pursuing another career besides marriage was beyond their thinking.

Eleanor Shatlock Markowitz's first and only job was in the metallurgy laboratory of the Homestead Works during World War II. A high school student then, she worked three shifts, testing ladles of steel to see if alloys needed to be added for final production. After working all night, she caught a bus for home, changed clothes, and headed for Divine Providence Academy, twelve miles and two trolleys away. "You know, you're young, and things just don't seem hard," she says with simplicity. "I just wanted to do something to help the war. It was all so new and exciting and challenging. I was never exposed to anything like that. I loved everything about the lab. The only bad part was the odor of dead rats when I had to walk through the old section of the mill."

Yet Eleanor never thought about going to college for a degree in chemistry. "I was just glad to have a little chance to know what it was like to work. It was a good experience for me. Lots of women didn't have that chance, or if they did, they worked in a store. But I wish I *had* stayed with a job of some sort. Men didn't think a woman should work back then. My husband didn't. We were married in 1945 when he was discharged from the service, and that was that."

Most steelworkers during the war were older married men. "But there were never any problems," Eleanor adds. "I never had any fears. Some of them, I suppose, were too friendly. Maybe we just didn't know it was a problem," she laughs.

Eleanor's social life was controlled by the shift she was working. "I'd be swimming with friends at Kennywood, and would have to leave. But that's just the way things had to be. Work was really my social life. Sometimes after a shift, I'd go out with some of the other girls for dessert."

But not all the Rosies were interested in ice-cream sodas and sundaes. Others preferred unwinding at neighborhood bars. This part of Rosie the Riveter's routine is seldom talked about. Steelworkers' wives didn't like it. One wife, now 86, described her feelings, but asked me not to use her name.

As I sat around a dining room table with her, her son Bill and his wife Diana, they all chatted helpfully about the rigorous demands on a steelworker's wife: laundering work clothes, cooking ethnic foods and preserving European holiday customs. When I asked Bill's mother about her memories of Rosie the Riveter, I expected to hear an outburst of patriotic pride in her gender. Instead, her lips tightened. Oblivious to his mother's rigid body language, Bill patiently explained to me how women left the mills and returned to domesticity after soldiers came back from the war to reclaim their jobs or start school on the GI Bill. His mother was clearly agitated.

So I repeated my question to her. "How *did* you feel about women working in the mill?"

"Women loved my husband," she begins. "They chased him so much that it made me angry that he wouldn't come straight home from work. He and his buddies would be at the bar and have such a good time. They'd drink and dance with the girls. And he'd tell me, 'Oh, so and so is such a good kid. She's a lot of fun.' I didn't want to hear that and got fed up."

From Bill's discomfort, I suspect he hadn't heard this story before.

Ignoring her son's chagrin, his mother shares her strategy: "So one day I got all dressed up with make-up, and I said, 'Mom, you watch the kids. Take care of them kids,' and I went to the bar. He was so surprised and kept kicking me under the table to keep my mouth shut.

"But I stayed around and got to know the women and invited them to my house for dinner. I had children then, and one girl came up to me and said, 'I don't flirt with him. I know he has a family.' But the others were flirting with him. In a few days, four of them came for dinner and when they got to see him with his children, they didn't chase after him as much. I wanted them to know there was this cute little house and I was a good cook."

Defensively, Bill wants to make sure I understand that his father never cheated on his mother: "That it was just a way of life."

"He liked the attention," his mother says with finality.

A retired steelworker had a different take on the relationships between men and women millworkers. The way men "disparaged the reputation" of women co-workers during World War II, "said they were 'loose'"—that bothered him, he told me. "There was always a lot of jostling and kidding, saying 'you should know about her,' or 'let me tell you'. . . but I never saw anything. Women worked hard. They wore hard shoes. My wife had a relative that worked in the mill, and I always felt sorry for what she was up against."

Even as they were being hired, women had to confront stereotypes about how they act and why. A special presentation, "Supervising the Working Woman," given on January 21, 1943 at the Duquesne Works, includes the following reminders and advice: ". . . the dislikes and likes of women are much deeper and much more venomous than the dislikes of men. . . . Women's [sic] thigh bones incline inwardly toward her knees [making] her more susceptible to tripping than a man [and lessening] her ability to balance herself easily. . . . Women admire men because they realize nature favors them. They have a desire to act like men and be treated as men. . . . Women are naturally clean as compared with men. There is no job a woman will attack with so much enthusiasm as she will cleaning up."

With this welcome, it's understandable why women were considered dispensable in the steel industry when the war ended in 1945. Yet the reality is that women wearing "hard shoes" kept up with men and contributed to the production of airplanes, tanks, warships, guns and ammunitions that helped the Allies win the war.

Adele Vamos called my attention to her interview with an anonymous ex-Rosie, published in *Out of This Kitchen* (1993). Like any man, she worked three shifts, six days a week at the Homestead Works. Her walk back and forth to the plant included a steep flight of seventy-five steps to her home high in the Homestead hills. "I started out on the labor gang pitching bricks from boxcars. . . . It was a fearful job because once the furnace would burn out, different groups . . . would clean [it] out. . . . They were only allowed in there for a few minutes. The bricks would burn down and they wouldn't work anymore. The fire was all gas and it was under a big pot. That's what it was like. I always said that when I die, I'll never go to hell because I was in hell for four years."

Although all women hired for the wartime effort had temporary status, the superintendent of the Duquesne Works, K. H. McLaurin, worried that they would refuse to leave their jobs, particularly if they had seniority over some of the younger men or veterans returning from the war. But according to Rose's study, the "wartime female production labor force of over 700 workers was reduced to 125" by June 1, 1946. A month later, only sixteen women remained in the Duquesne Works, all working in the metallurgical or chemical laboratories rather than on the mill floors.

"After the war, Edgar Thomson got rid of women right away," Jim Boland says approvingly. "But Homestead kept them and so did Ohio Works. One woman worked for me when I was up there. Oh, I dreaded to be on daylight with her. Pain in the ass."

Women staying in this unwelcome environment potentially earned the same seniority and benefits as men, but supervisors were often crafty in setting up obstacles. Furthermore, Rosie the Riveters seeking other employment became locked in low-paying jobs like store clerks and waitresses. A critical turning point occurred in April 1974, though, when nine of the nation's largest steel companies signed a "Consent Decree," settling a suit filed by the Equal Employment Opportunity Commission (EEOC), the U.S. Department of Justice, and the Labor Department. An important part of the Consent Decree provides that steel companies and the USWA hire women and minorities for half the openings in trade and craft jobs plus twenty-five percent of the vacancies in the supervisory positions. The decree also forced the mills to make changes in the seniority system, which got women and minorities into better paying, more desirable jobs, with healthcare plans.

Women college students also benefited from the Consent Decree because it allowed them the same options young men had for summer jobs in steel plants. They could now work in production rather than fill gofer positions in food service or offices. Between terms at Penn State in 1980, Paula Kurtz worked on the floor of the Homestead plant, the "scariest, worst and best job I ever had." Even though she grew up within sight of the mill, she had "no context for what was inside. It's very frightening: all fire and noise."

She was assigned to the structural mill of the Homestead Works, one of the most dangerous areas because newly pressed steel beams spilled off rollers and swung overhead while "hookers" attached them to cranes transporting them to various destinations. As a "slip maker," Paula was assigned to decode the markings made by inspectors on the huge beams as they rolled to the end of the production line. "The beams zipped all around, and then were stacked. I had to crawl around them, up and down, reading the markings with a flashlight to see if they could move on somewhere else or had to be shipped back to be hammered out."

Some of the hieroglyphics Paula decoded identified the steelworker who had pressed each beam. Because bonuses and incentives were determined by the number of successful beams pressed, she never wanted to make a mistake with the paints—"yellow and orange, I think"—she carried with her to mark the beams with her own code.

To tally her figures for the accounting office, she retreated to a "shanty, like a little metal house, 10 by 8 feet that had a desk for me to do my paperwork." Because the shanty was on the production floor, Paula still had to wear her goggles and security hat. "I always had to be alert and attentive because you could be electrocuted or hit by a beam flying overhead," she explains.

Yet the hardest part of the job for Paula was not having the respect of senior women steelworkers. "The men were fine. Except for one time a man jumped out at me and said he'd like to lick off my lipgloss. The men helped me out and showed me how to be careful, but the women were tough and foul-mouthed. And I'm not sure why."

Paula generally worked double shifts, then slept, and went back to work. But because women bullied her about claiming a locker, she'd leave the mill wearing her greasy jeans, shirt and boots. Sometimes she was badgered about using the toilet. "I was so dirty I didn't want to get into a car after work, but I didn't want to complain and bring more attention to myself." Nonetheless, Paula ends our conversation assuring me, "It was a great experience."

One of the most unusual women to benefit from the Consent Decree is Steffi Domike, who graduated from Reed College in 1976 as an economics major and student body president. Then she came east from Oregon to Pittsburgh to work at the Clairton Coke Works, starting as a janitor in the coke ovens, the first woman to hold that job.

"Why do this?" I kept asking.

"My parents are still wondering what I was doing," says Steffi. "It's not easy to explain or understand," but she gives it a try. She majored in economics because she wanted to understand "what made the world the way it is; how come there are rich people and why there are poor people, and why it doesn't seem to get better. I didn't take the usual route of a masters and a Ph.D. I was interested in learning about the U.S. labor movement from within, and so I wanted to get a job in industry to do that. Pittsburgh was the oldest steel center still hiring, but more important, it's the historical center of the labor movement."

So Pittsburgh seemed to be the right place for Steffi. "There was no indication at the time that the steel industry in this area would take such a big hit in the 1980s," she says. If she hadn't been one of the many laid off in October 1981, she might still be there.

"I'm a person of staying power, and the mill filled out my education. I had been raised in a world of books and ideas, but the mill gave me a better sense of how ideas are also stratified. How working people are really just as smart as academics; that it's not about intelligence but about having an opportunity. For health reasons alone," she concludes, "I'm glad I'm not there because of the high rate of cancer among coke workers."

Steffi's introspection seems appropriate as we sit at a wrought-iron table underneath a tree ablaze with red autumn leaves, on the bucolic campus of Chatham College, where she is an assistant professor and director of the digital technology program. The juxtaposition between the idyllic setting and Steffi's description of her first day on the floor at the USX Clairton Works is dramatic.

"People were camouflaged by protective devices and looked like aliens. It was totally surreal, and the colors were black and white and this deep, red orange," Steffi remembers. "When you walk into the coke oven it's like being in a city, but it's a city in your nightmare because the ovens are 100-feet tall and they're spewing this ghastly yellow stuff, and always leaking. There are fumes, and sounds of things backing up all the time. You have to watch out because equipment is pushing coal into the oven and trucks are always coming along. I felt completely lost. I'd like someday to try to recreate the experience of that."

Despite Steffi's use of Armageddon imagery, I'm reminded of what John Updike in *The Centaur* calls the "young colors of optimism."

Arriving at the coke plant in August 1976, she saw vestiges of the old hierarchical system and ethnic enclaves. "There was not only racial and sexual discrimination but also the ethnic divisions had historic roots. All the Blacks were in the production side of the coke works, which has the greatest health hazard and hardest physical labor. The Italians were the bricklayers. The Polish people were in the tin shop. The English or the Johnny Bulls were in the electric trades. The poor Irish or the poor rural whites were treated like the Blacks and confined to the lousy jobs. But the consent act freed everybody to bid over to other jobs, and you could start to see the results."

Steffi was happy to begin as a janitor rather than as a worker cleaning the railroad tracks, the other entry-level job. Although Clairton had been hiring women since 1974, men were still assigned to cleaning the women's bathrooms and "would simply lock the door and sleep, leaving the women with no place to go," Steffi says. But by 1976 when she signed on, Clairton saw the need to expand janitorial services. "I was lucky because it wasn't too bad a job, and I wasn't restricted to one particular place but got a chance to work all over the mill and understand what was going on."

After nine months, Steffi got a bid to the wire gang and was an electrician's apprentice for almost five years before being laid off. She's proud of knowing how to "wire up a house. I can take apart equipment and figure out how to put it back together. I learned to do the kind of work that women had been excluded from. And it was the older guys who were no longer studs that taught us to do the work."

Older men losing their physical strength had to figure out how to use their balance and weight in new ways if they wanted to continue in the trade. By observing and listening to them, Steffi claims women were able to learn how to maximize their own muscle and use work tools to their best advantage. "This doesn't mean there wasn't a lot of sexism on all levels," she quickly adds.

Steffi started an activist group called "Women of Steel." She brought together women in plants all up and down the Steel Valley. They shared problems, gave advice, organized a successful women's conference, and published the *Women of Steel Newsletter*. "Snappy Answers to Stupid Questions" is a feature in one issue: "Part of working in the mills is getting along with your fellow workers," the advice begins. "[Our] purpose is not to train every woman millworker to be a ball-buster or to hate men in any way. Its purpose, however, is to encourage women to defend our rights to our jobs. Sometimes you have the time for a long discussion or explanation about why you, as a woman, have chosen to enter the 'man's' world of heavy industry. Sometimes you just have time for a snappy reply. . . . Here are some of those replies that 'I wish I'd thought of.'"

> *Remark: Hey, do you fool around?*
> *Responses: 1. Are you a fool? 2. I don't fool around. I play for keeps and I don't think you can handle it.*

> *Remark: How about a little smile?*
> *Responses: 1. Sure, at quitting time on Friday. 2. Sometimes I just can't get it up.*

Facing the fact that women steelworkers would be the first to be laid off in 1981-82 because of having the lowest seniority, Steffi had to "think about other things to do, what to get involved in, and how to help others to act offensively." She became the first chairperson of the Mon Valley Unemployed Steelworkers Committee, organizing food banks and hassling communities to think creatively about helping the unemployed. For herself, she finished a degree in photography and multimedia and launched a new career in filmmaking, producing *River Run Red*, a re-creation of the Homestead Strike of 1892, filmed at the Pinkerton landing site, and *Women of Steel*, a documentary she made with three other women in 1985 about women hired in the 1970s having to return to low-paying jobs after being permanently laid off by the steel plants.

"No sooner were women in the mill than they were out the door. They were the last ones in and the first ones out," says Mike Stout, a union grievance officer at the Homestead Works during the same time Steffi Domike was in Clairton.

But in their brief history, beginning with the tin lines, women steelworkers charted new territory—addressing issues, asking questions, creating problems—by straying from the conventional paths women were expected to travel.

Chapter 7

✦✦✦

Mill Kids' Memories

It was a rich experience. No one thought about being poor.

One of my unexpected pleasures in talking with men and women of the Steel Valley was listening to their memories of growing up as mill kids, and how they treasure early images. Their recollections are mostly nostalgic, for time often gives a magical glow to youth, despite deprivation and hardship.

Artists Anna Marie Sninsky and Bob Qualters were inspired by their earliest visual memories of the mills. For them, the mills were never about poverty and dirt, but texture, color and narrative. Walking home in the wintertime, up the steep hill from St. Michael's, the Slovak school in Homestead, Sninsky saw graphite "sparkling like diamonds" on new fallen snow, instead of grime coating it black.

One of her paintings, an acrylic 6 by 4 feet, shows three women waiting outside a steel mill. Their heads covered with black babushkas, two of them huddle together under an umbrella in secretive silence. A third woman, straight and tall, wearing a black cloche and high button shoes, stands by herself, a figure of mystery.

The painting dramatizes a scene common to the public memory of the Steel Valley. Wives were always waiting outside the mills on payday to collect their husbands' wages before men spent them on gambling, booze or prostitution. But Sninsky has a more private memory of a woman, walking up and down the hills, always alone. She never spoke nor came very near, until the day, decades later, when she strolled onto Sninsky's canvas.

Bob Qualters is known for his paintings of the steel mills, their neighborhoods and urban landscapes. The Carnegie Museum of Art owns a Qualters as do many corporate offices across the United States. We talked in his fourth-floor studio in Homestead, parallel to where the Homestead Works once sprawled. At the time, the Andy Warhol Museum had an exhibit of his work. Qualters graduated from Carnegie Tech (now Carnegie Mellon University) a few years after Warhol.

As a child, he attended St. Joseph School, right above the Clairton Coke Works. "We'd stand out in front of the school and look down a very steep hill that went right into the mills. We'd say the "Pledge of Allegiance" and the smoke would come out sulfurous pink, smelling like little boys breaking wind. Who knew how poisonous it was? We never thought about it."

In the summertime, Qualters and his friends swam in a pool across from immense coal mines that were "hot as hell. All those images become part of you, whether you want them or not."

Qualters never cared about how steel was made; he cared about how it affected the color of everything. "How could I forget what night looked like when the furnaces were working and the whole sky would turn red and pulsate, often with snow coming down? The light would bounce right off the side of the cliffs when they had almost no vegetation."

But it didn't require an artist's eye to appreciate such radiance. The favorite amusement of the Millers growing up was to lounge on a blanket while eating ice-cream cones on a hill across from the "Devil's Graveyard," a slag heap for the steel plants. The sky turned fiery red, "like the Fourth of July," when slag was dumped. "That was our fun. Can you imagine kids being satisfied with that now?" Millie rolls her eyes.

The wonder of slag heaps is a shared experience in the Steel Valley. Looking like dragons and devils pouring down from the stars, slag had both the aura of myth and cheap entertainment.

Before becoming a steelworker, Charles Stewart connected the blazing sky with romance. As a teenager during the '30s, he sat on a hill with dates, watching the sky light up, silently thinking about his father, who hauled liquid slag from the mills on the Union Railroad. "I'd be proud imagining my father dumping the slag, painting the sky. It was so spectacular."

Feelings of pride and patriotism in their fathers' work stay with mill kids long after leaving their family homes. A New York editor, Mary Ann Eckels, told me about her father working at Pittsburgh-Des Moines, a plant that fabricated steel for the World Trade Center. She has strong images of him visiting the construction sight of the Twin Towers in 1969 and walking on the high beams. "Now I keep thinking about his fingerprints being on some of them." During World War II, she watched ships and submarines being launched from Neville Island, five miles west of downtown Pittsburgh. She imagined them traveling down the Ohio and Mississippi, out to the Gulf, and across to Europe.

On the day of a launch, the families of workers, waving flags and playing Sousa marches felt special, a community contributing to the war effort. But the water surrounding Neville Island was always a "luminous blue and green and glowed in the dark. We didn't want to think of what made it glow—maybe mercury," Mary Ann laughs. Most nights, she had trouble falling asleep because of the bright sky. She teases that one of her sisters still feels most comfortable in Alaska or Norway. When the family moved further up the river, Mary Ann missed the loud noises of the mill. "They were constant but rhythmic, and it was hard to get used to the silence."

These booming sounds were lullabies to generations of kids growing up within the range of blast furnaces. One of them, now vice-president of the Homestead and Mifflin Township Historical Society, talked to me in his tiny archival office in the rear of the Carnegie Library of Homestead, only a few blocks from the site of the 1892 Battle of Homestead. One wouldn't suspect John Hartman, a burly man and retired mail carrier, of harboring much sentiment, but he has a strong sense of place, a vital talent for any historian. His father, a steelworker, moved the family away from the Duquesne Works to an area "more like country, where there were still farms and not much traffic during the '50s and early '60s." Adapting was not easy for John. He missed Duquesne, "down by the mill here you'd have whistles blowing, this blowing, that blowing, trains going by . . . what do you call that? Comfort noises? Yeah, comfort noises."

Seventy years ago, Anna Mae Vamos lived about as close to the Homestead plant as anyone could. After the midnight shift, she and her sisters sneaked through their bedroom window onto a flat garage roof where their mother fermented bottles of homemade rootbeer. Giddy from drinking, they fell asleep under the red heavens, soothed by clanging noises, the metronome of the mill.

Very few mill kids ever saw the inside of a steel plant, but they knew what was happening by the sounds they heard. "You knew when they were unloading the steel off the rolls," said Adele Vamos, 50, Anna Mae's daughter. "It had a rhythm to it. You could count on it. Trains. Boats. Foghorns. Nothing is as therapeutic and consistent as steel mill sounds."

"It wasn't until you moved away and had other experiences that you realized everyone didn't live that way, and that was so freeing to learn," Reverend Tom Bonacci told me. Before he left for seminary, he remembers saying his prayers, looking from his bedroom window down into the fiery furnaces of the Duquesne Works.

Mill kids lived in a predictable but not protective, world. Death, violence and strikes were part of daily life. Growing up, Yvonne Godbolt knew that her father's leg had been amputated in a mill accident while her mother was pregnant with her. As a child, she worried about "danger all the time," because the Homestead plant posted signs about how many days had occurred since the last accident, and her brothers were steelworkers.

Living through strikes and layoffs was tough for mill kids. Too proud to stand in line for handouts of "welfare cheese," powdered milk and stale bread, parents often sent their children to cart home what they could. But mill kids endured the hardship of strikes because they believed unions were trying to do better for their families. Even in the darkest days, Joanne Karaczun's father reminded her, "If it wasn't for the union, we wouldn't be eating." The Miller sisters exchanged teary glances: "Dad never ate until all of us were finished." A son remembers his father refusing to drink milk in order to save it for the kids, and his mother keeping a tin bank on a kitchen shelf to save against the next strike.

"Families were always watching pennies 'because there's going to be a strike,'" Bonnie Harvey told me in her office at the Carnegie Library of Homestead. "Taft-Hartley was a very real thing to me as a fifth-grader because I knew what that meant. We always talked issues and politics at Sunday dinner with my grandparents. S*trike* and *layoff* weren't just textbook words to me."

At a young age, poverty and prejudice were realities to mill kids. Although ethnic and religious diversity was generally respected in mill neighborhoods by the end of World War II, newcomers from Europe, seeking work in the mills in the early twentieth century settled with their own kind, close to German, Irish, Slovak or Polish churches and grade schools. Children started first grade speaking a European tongue and knowing little English.

I talked with Pat French at the oldest Bulgarian Center in the United States, founded in Homestead seventy-five years ago. On Saturday mornings, customers come from all over Pittsburgh to buy quarts of homemade mushroom and lentil soups. The present center, built in 1932, was once open seven days a week for 800 families wanting to maintain their heritage and culture, and yet learn American ways. Only men were granted membership to the club, but women did the work, Pat told me. As a little girl, Pat saw her mother and other women cooking for Bulgarian steelworkers who hung out at the center, hoping to marry Bulgarian girls.

As she tidied up after the morning soup sales, Pat told me that "shut up" was the only English phrase she knew as a six-year-old starting first grade. When the teacher asked her name, Pat answered, "Shut Up." Everyone in her class spoke a different language—Russian, Croatian, Hungarian, Bulgarian. From the cacophony of sound, first-grade teachers eventually produced English-speaking children. "But we learned ethnic slurs very early," Pat said. "Kids taunted each other with names."

When Chuck Prezmonti's parents moved further away from the Edgar Thomson plant into a Johnny Bull neighborhood, kids wouldn't play with him and called him a hunky.

But mill kids generally undercut their memories of prejudice and poverty with irony and sometimes sentiment. I watched the eyes of a stalwart octogenarian, a retired steelworker, as he described roaming wheatfields and cornfields as a boy in Slovakia before crossing the ocean to live in a house smack up against the steel mill where his father worked. "The kids called me a *greenhorn*," he remembers his hurt as a ten-year-old. "We were all steelworkers' kids, but they happened to be born here. I looked up the word *greenhorn* and realized I knew more about this country than they did because of my reading. *Greenhorn*. That word stayed with me. But we had an outside privy with a door on it, one you could lock. And that was something!"

Mill kids of all ages temper any hint of self-pity with humor. "We were high-class. We had screens on our windows," one man said about growing up as a mill kid in the '60s. "We'd stand on porches and look through screen doors to see television," a woman told me who can't remember ever leaving McKeesport as a child except to visit grandparents in New Castle. "But we always celebrated birthdays with a big cake," she said. "Our neighbors had pie for dessert on Sunday night, and I thought that was really great!"

For mill kids, entertainment centered on religious holidays, family customs and ethnic food. "It was a colorful life for kids," says Anna Marie Sninsky. "Slovaks, Italians, Jews—we celebrated everybody's holiday. We'd see the Easter baskets prepared by the Byzantines and the twelve-fish dinners the Italians served on Christmas Eve. We were all in and out of each other's houses. Gypsy bands played for weddings and funerals. It was a rich experience. No one thought about being poor."

In early autumn, Slovak families began getting ready for Christmas Eve dinner by chopping cabbage for sour mushroom soup. Martha Sloan remembers her older brothers sitting across from each other with a big clothes basket between them, covered with a clean tablecloth. Each grasped a handle of a large piece of wood with embedded blades to cut the cabbage heads in half. Then the boys pushed the saw back and forth catching the cabbage slivers in the cloth before dumping them into big earthen crocks and squishing the cabbage with their bare feet to make sauerkraut. The juice was a major ingredient for the soup to be served on Christmas Eve.

As a child, Helen Havrilla, now 88, walked miles with her parents on Sunday afternoons to visit other steelworking families to exchange vegetables they had grown in their gardens. "It was just ordinary food, but what we didn't eat, we'd preserve. We'd survive the winter on pickles, carrots and corn." What Helen enjoyed most was listening to the women talk while they canned. "It was comfortable because the children would play and help too. We didn't think about being poor because we thought everybody was like us," she shrugs.

Over the decades, Sunday and holiday traditions changed little for mill kids. Church in the morning and a big family dinner at one o'clock with grandparents, uncles and aunts. "Sunday rest was relative," comments Mary Jo Bensasi, aware of gender differences as a teenager in the '70s. "Somebody still had to prepare the meal." Her maternal Italian grandmother spent all morning cooking meatballs and sauce, pasta, fried chicken and salad. Then the women and girls did the dishes. For holidays at her Slovakian grandparents' home, getting ready to play penny ante poker was the priority for the men. "They'd rush the women to hurry up and serve the food so the table could be cleared for playing cards. There were so many people we had to eat in shifts around a dining room table that seated ten people."

As I talked with women at the same tables where they had once served so many meals, I saw family pictures displayed like little shrines on dining room walls. Most prevalent were restored photographs of children wearing their First Communion dresses, veils or suits. In May, in honor of Mary, the mother of Jesus, little girls loved walking to school in fancy white dresses decorated with religious medals and flowing ribbons. By the time they arrived, their dresses were covered with soot from the mills. When a child died, a funeral director would often mount the open coffin on a horse-drawn carriage and process through town, the child dressed in First Communion clothes, or, in the case of Martha Sloan's brother, a little soldier suit.

On boring Sunday afternoons, Bonnie Harvey and her friends would visit the numerous ethnic Catholic churches, outwait the stragglers from Mass, and light all the vigil candles protected in red glass jars. For her first college theme, Bonnie wrote about her Twelfth Avenue block "because it was so diverse, but we didn't use that term then." Czech, Jewish and Irish families "had an open, sharing relationship. It wasn't unusual to say 'come and see how to make pasta or gefilte fish or pierogies.'"

The five Miller sisters told me they were baptized Methodist because their Serbian Orthodox mother and Lutheran father saw it as a reasonable compromise. As little girls, they attended services at the Serbian church, the Catholic church, and the synagogue. They prayed the rosary and implored St. Jude for hopeless cases.

Their mother often sent them to a Catholic parish to light candles and bring home holy water. When their brother William returned from World War II with water from Lourdes, every family in the neighborhood was given a vial with instructions to say a prayer. Their mother's Jewish butcher asked to offer a prayer at their father's funeral. "We thought it was wonderful," the sisters agreed. "Diversity was natural to us."

After learning about the sacrament of Baptism in her second-grade class at St. Brendan's School in Braddock, during World War II, a woman recalls lining up her little Jewish friends and baptizing them with tap water from Sal and Eugene Litman's kitchen sink.

Christmas was often the best and worst of times for steelworkers' families, but kids celebrated with very little. For their first Christmas in this country as young children, Mary Soncini remembers her brother, John Hrika, bringing home a discarded, bottom branch from an evergreen tree. "In Europe we would hang a small tree from the ceiling and put candles on it, so we hung these few branches from the ceiling and decorated them with ten tiny little bulbs that our mother managed to buy for us, and I still have. That was the way we had Christmas. But I guess you survive. You do."

For Adele Vamos, the best part of being a steelworker's daughter was the children's Christmas parties given by fraternal organizations. "Most steelworkers belonged to the Vets or Eagles, and they gave the best presents," Adele reminisced in her mother's kitchen, the home where she grew up. "We'd get bags of fruit and candy and coloring books and crayons, which was a lot for us then." John Hrika still talks about an orange he was given at a Red Cross Christmas party. "This orange was so tasty. I still haven't come across one like it."

Life was so "drab and grim" for Sandy Haas Doby, 48, as a steelworker's daughter, that she still cherishes a Santa Claus, with thinning beard and worn red suit, she found in her Christmas stocking as a seven-year-old. He is one of over a thousand Santa Clauses she now displays in her home, three hundred sixty-eight of which she has painted by hand. She began collecting and painting Santa Clauses when her husband, Jinx, worked night turn at the Irvin Works. "I was bored," she acknowledges. "What do you do when your husband's working and the kids are in bed? I couldn't leave them. My mother cleaned, but I paint Santa Clauses."

It's July, but a ceramic Santa Claus spoon rests on her stove, next to Mr. and Mrs. Claus salt and pepper shakers, tea towels, calendars and mugs with Santa handles. A two-foot Santa in royal velvet robes presides on the living room mantel. A train toots around the carpet, searching for a Christmas tree. Not one inch of space, from floor to ceiling, is without an image of Santa, Mrs. Claus, an elf or reindeer. One Santa soaks his feet in water, another stuffs his backpack with toys. Santa Claus, the acrobat, dangles from the ceiling. Mrs. Claus, the ballerina, flirts across the room. The Santa Claus industry has been picked clean. Why?

Sandy's father, Ted Haas, died as a result of a mill accident when she was very young, leaving seven children. Except for the Santa she found in her stocking, Sandy says her childhood had little color, few surprises. So she keeps collecting and painting Santa Clauses because they make her "smile and feel happy. I like to touch them."

Mill kids expected little entertainment. Little girls were pleased when their mothers sewed new outfits for their dolls from remnants of material. Little boys always played dangerous games and treated railroad tracks as a playground. They competed with each other to fill baskets with coal chips that fell from passing rail cars. But the real point of the game was to collect fuel for their homes. Kids also scrambled for flares from the railroad tracks to sell the lead at the dump for spending money. "Lead! Can you imagine?" Mary Cvetan exclaimed about her grandfather's idea of fun. "No wonder he lost his mind."

In her grandfather's time, row houses were often built around a courtyard, which had a drain in the middle where families washed their dishes and took baths. Wooden clapboard enclosures offered some privacy around tubs. A favorite pastime of kids was to see how many slivers of soap they could pry off the drain because they could be molded and used again. The leftover soap was precious and the rivalry was fun.

Venturesome mill kids poked around the streets near the railroad tracks for other reasons than collecting coal. The red-light district in steel towns was usually parallel to the railroad and close to the entrance of the steel plant. "We were kids, but we'd see these blondes, all dressed up, getting out of cabs, being dropped off," said Anna Mae Vamos, 79, "and we'd see the men going into the different places. We never saw anything specific, but we knew what was goin' on. We used to go to a baker shop right around the corner from Evelyn Marshall's place," which was called the Chapel in Homestead. "It was a church for the guys, I guess," cracks Anna Mae. "We'd also watch from our windows at home, and we'd see guys knocking, and the women would say, 'come on in.' Cars came from everywhere on weekends."

As a boy, Joe Chioda, 80, swept the floor at his father's shoemaking shop, a Homestead landmark, but had the eye of a cultural anthropologist when it came to women's shoes. He could spot the prostitutes because "they always wore the finest shoes—real top-grade leather—and they were always very nice to me."

As a delivery boy in the late '20s and early '30s, Raymond Stevens carried groceries to "The Chapel," but he never "saw the women smoking cigarettes, or saying 'damn' or saw clothes in disarray. They were prostituting to keep families together," he told me while downing a beer after a union meeting for old-time steelworkers at the Homestead Elks.

Mill kids always "giggled over the cathouses," says Bonnie Harvey. On Sunday afternoons when sixth- and seventh-graders took long walks, they ignored their parents' order to keep away from Sixth and Seventh Avenues, the red-light district.

But it's the safety and color of their neighborhoods that mill kids mostly remember. "Everyone kept their doors and windows open, and looked out for each other," Anne Pcholinsky, 78, enjoyed telling me while adjusting her cardigan sweater that matches her ash-blond hair. "There were always nice aromas coming from the houses. Everybody's place on Fleet Street in Rankin smelled from tomato sauce or sweet peppers cooking. But on Third Street you'd smell stuffed cabbage on

Saturdays or breaded veal and chicken on Sunday mornings. You'd still smell the cooking in church, and I'd think 'let Mass be over.' I want to run home and eat."

Joseph "Red" Szwarc, a retired barber, liked walking on Talbot Avenue, near the Edgar Thomson plant when he was a boy because of the cooking odors coming from the houses. One block would be Slovak, another Italian, another Lithuanian.

A favorite neighborhood of kids was the Ward, the six-square block area near the Homestead Works that had cheap housing, ethnic churches, fraternal organizations and grocery stores. As families prospered, they moved up into the hills overlooking the steel plant. Others were displaced when the federal government bought and dismantled properties in 1941 so that the Homestead Works could expand to increase production for World War II.

"I was born in 1927 and was crushed to leave that wonderful neighborhood," Millie Tarasevich, the hardworking owner of Straka's Tavern, told me while drinking hot tea at her dining room table on a wintry Sunday afternoon. "It was during the Depression that we all drew close. Everybody was just family. We just loved and took care of each other."

A popular joke about the Ward is that if one house got a roach, they all did. Anna Mae Vamos lived for twenty-one years with her parents and eleven siblings, most of whom she saw born, in a four-room house. Their kitchen window was so close to the mill that if she were home from school at noon, she could watch steelworkers unpacking their lunch buckets. Workers sometimes beckoned kids to bring them extra drinks or cakes from the store. "But we were always safe. It wasn't like today," Anna Mae adds. Little girls played outdoor games at night, and "our brothers watched us so that nothing would happen. There were seldom any fights because no one had reason to get mad at each other."

A highlight for little girls was watching the "corset lady." Women in the Ward had "big bellies from having all those kids so she'd come a few times a year and measure them in their houses. They were pretty tight, too," Anna Mae describes. "They had all these strings in them that you tied here and over there," she twists from side to side to demonstrate.

So many of the Ward people are dead, she laments, but enough are around to recognize each other while shopping and eating at the Waterfront, where the Ward houses once stood. "We still have a feeling for each other. Even now, people will say to me, 'you're one of the Bernd girls.'"

Homes were razed not only in the Ward, but also near the railroad tracks in Duquesne, to build a steel plant before World War II. People who lived there have "below-the-track reunions," Lorraine Novak told me. "They're really proud and come from all over, but I went to one and felt like an outsider," she confesses, "because I lived up by the water tank. If you didn't live below the tracks, people would just say, 'oh,' and walk away from me."

Hilltop streets in Steel Valley towns evoke different images from the mean streets around the mills. "If you went down the hill to other people's houses with a strong ethnic background, there was a lot more dimension to things," observes Robert Gibb, who grew up in Homestead during the '60s. He'd sneak out to the house next-door to have lunch with workmen because he could get a "baloney sandwich on black bread, whereas at home it was all nice white bread. You really didn't have to have the income to be confined to a world of affectation. Working-class people tend to be more open, more gregarious, warm and emotional, and less concerned about status and elbowing for who's coming out on top."

Gibb didn't have these insights as a mill kid, but time is not mechanical, he points out. Moments that are the deepest keep flowing in and out of memory, turning up in unexpected ways, influencing the present, touching the imagination.

Coda

◆✦◆

What Remains

Only one thing is entirely clear about the closing of the steel mills and subsidiary plants in Southwestern Pennsylvania during the 1980s: they died a slow death. The complex causes of the closings included a decline in manufacturing jobs that began during the economic recession of the '70s; the expense of upgrading old equipment to comply with new environmental and safety regulations; foreign entry into the once-safe steel market; advanced technology that required fewer unskilled workers; demands by the unions for higher pay and more vacation time; sloppy and lazy work habits; global markets and cheaper overseas labor.

"Nobody thought it was actually happening," Betty Esper told me. An office employee at U. S. Steel Homestead for thirty-six years, she remembers that, "You saw it slowing down but you didn't think they would really go out of business. Just like an apple. It just rotted and rotted and rotted until there was no more apple. . . . So that was it. When I walked out, drove out of the mill for the last time, there was nobody left to even say good-bye to. There were some security guards, but they weren't company men, just hired outsiders."

Today, a memorial marker locked inside a wire cage tangled with weeds and stray plastic flowers sits on Braddock Avenue near the main entrance of Edgar Thomson "in memory of employees of the Edgar Thomson plant who lost their lives while on the job. You are not forgotten," it says.

This marble plaque was dedicated in 1997, some seventy-five years after Father Kazincy, near the same spot, rallied families to protest brutalities within the mill, and ninety years after my grandfather was killed when he fell into the Thomson rollers.

The memorial was my final stop on a blustery January day after I had toured the Mon Valley Works, three plants still operated by U. S. Steel: Clairton, Irvin, and ET. In comparison to the stories of the people I had talked with, the words of the marker seemed trite, and its shabby appearance betrayed any promise of truly honoring the lives of those who had died while making steel.

By visiting these surviving plants, I had expected to be transported to an earlier time, to experience viscerally what it was like to walk in my grandfather's shoes. But instead of feeling connected, I felt detached. The buildings at Edgar Thomson were the same ones built by Andrew Carnegie, but the grounds and interiors were eerie in their emptiness. Walking through the gates, I felt trapped in grey fog and bleak silence. The only signs of life were in glass-enclosed rooms high above the production floor. At this safe distance, men studying floor-to-ceiling computer controls punched keys that regulated the chemical processes for making steel. Others stared at desk-sized monitors that spewed messages. Classical music filled the air at one computer station. An overhead crane glided quietly past the window. A few workers dressed like robots looked ready for a moonwalk. "Do you work shifts?" I asked one of them. Behind his goggles, he looked askance. "It would be pretty hard," he sniffed, "for a dual-career couple."

Even though I had heard about ET's high performance technology, I still felt like Rip Van Winkle waking up in a new age, or a Kafka character alienated from modern life. In the deep silence of the mill's cavernous interior, I stifled an urge to yell, "What's going on here?" until I stood only yards away from the mammoth blast furnace, and I knew where I was again.

The 2006 steel plant was freezing cold, but the 2,700-degree internal heat of the blast furnace made my face feel as if I were standing at the edge of a volcano. Four men, wearing aluminum safety suits, were preparing to tap the furnace to release and separate the slag and molten iron churning inside. With the speed of an Alpine avalanche, silver liquid tumbled into a cauldron fit to be stirred by Macbeth's three witches. Vesuvian noises and orgiastic colors erupted. In counterpoint, millions of brilliant metal chips floated delicately, coating my steel hat, security glasses and probably my lungs. More volcanic sounds exploded, and yellow, blue and red flames soared when a massive ladle dumped the molten iron into the basic oxygen furnace in preparation for the rolling mill to shape it into slabs or billets of steel.

I witnessed this spectacle of sound, light and heat while standing in the deepest recess of Edgar Thomson. Only there, at the very heart of the plant, did I finally understand that the process of making steel has remained basically the same since the early days of the industry. Until then, I neither saw nor sensed the drama that steelworkers had told me about, for the new technology that is so visible in the plant disguises its elemental danger.

It was rare for people of the Steel Valley ever to see the inside of a working plant. It still is. "Not even Mrs. Carnegie got this close," said my guide, Timothy E. Quinn, the plant supervisor.

All the more reason to safeguard the living words of steelworkers and their families before their world completely disappears, leaving us only artificial flowers and false promises.